MARK DANDO is a mento   d
Coloured Square with Doug   ey
have used their very particul   nt
to provide help for people and org   nt,
leadership, sales, field management, influence, presenting, and ng,
training design…in fact, in anything that involves communication.

Well-being and resilience have been common themes in Mark and Doug's work for nearly twenty years, but in the last two years they've been pulling together many strands and principles to provide a single package which will address the topic more formally.

Don't Strain LittleBrain demanded to be written as a result.

It is Mark's third book. The first two, written with Doug, are about their attitudes to time and to presenting.

Mark lives in Bristol. He recently published his first children's book, *The Boy Who Yawned*, also with SilverWood Books. His friends think he reads a lot. His kids think he plays a lot. His guitar teacher knows he doesn't practise enough. He keeps himself pretty busy. He's trying to learn to chill out a bit more.

Maybe this book will help.

To find out more visit the Coloured Square website at www.colouredsquare.com.

Also by Mark Dando with Doug Richardson

Squeeze Your Time
Kill the Robot

Children's books by Mark Dando

The Boy Who Yawned

Don't Strain LittleBrain

■ A Mindset Book ■

Mark Dando

SilverWood

Published in 2017 by SilverWood Books

SilverWood Books Ltd
14 Small Street, Bristol, BS1 1DE, United Kingdom
www.silverwoodbooks.co.uk

ISBN 978-1-78132-699-2 (paperback)
ISBN 978-1-78132-700-5 (ebook)

British Library Cataloguing in Publication Data
A CIP catalogue record for this book is available from the British Library

Page design and typesetting by SilverWood Books
Printed on responsibly sourced paper

Contents

Introduction

Work leaves me frazzled – once I'm done,
I don't have the energy for anything else

I've too much information to get
through – I'm cc-ed on everything

There's too much to do – I struggle to
keep up and I feel out of control

All I want to do when I get home
after work is to sit on the sofa

Even if I had time, I'm just too tired
to have a life at the moment

I don't have time to think. I don't have time to plan

Just when I'm getting on top, I'm asked to do more

It's this job – if I worked somewhere else
I'd have a better work/life balance

I don't have time to enjoy myself

I hear these kinds of mindsets a lot. When I'm working with people on their sense of well-being or resilience, these kinds of statements come up very quickly.

There's a reason we don't have the kind of life we want, a life where we don't feel so frazzled after work that we can still make all our goals happen, a life where we're not too tired to enjoy ourselves.

> It takes hard work not to get frazzled

> Staying resourceful is difficult

> Enjoying your life isn't easy – it takes effort

> There's just too much to balance in a balanced life: I can't do it all

> It takes more effort than expected to keep on it and create the year I want

> It feels easier to chill out on the sofa than to create the life you really want

> I don't have time to work on me (so I don't get frazzled) and still have time to enjoy life

There – I've said it now! Not very inspiring, is it? Not so calming – not increasing your well-being! Not even the kind of thing that should be said in a book about well-being!

Ah, well. As usual, if you were looking for a touchy-feely book about the magical secrets of life, in which all it takes is a wish, a dream, or a positive attitude and everything will be different, this is going to be the wrong book for you. There are plenty of those available – just do a quick search online and order one of those instead.

By contrast, in this one, we'll take a *realistic* look at the kind of tricky choices you'll need to make every day of the week (sometimes every hour of the day). We'll look at how difficult they are, despite the fact they make so much sense. This will help you reconsider the way you think about your role, your life, your time, yourself – so you have a better chance of doing a few simple but significant things to improve your resilience and well-being.

Over a number of years of adopting deliberate ways of working and organising myself to increase my resilience and reduce the level of frazzle, I've noticed it does take a lot of energy and effort to live life in the way I want, to enjoy life during the week, when I'm working hard, maybe working long hours – even to enjoy life at the weekend when I feel like I've exhausted myself through the week and I've nothing left.

But, crucially, if I know this, then it helps – it makes it more likely I can make the right choices at the right moments, difficult though they are.

This book is for you, if...

You want to use this awareness to start to do things differently.

You want to understand why it's so difficult to avoid getting frazzled.

You'd like to feel more energised more often.

You don't want to wait until the weekends or your holidays to enjoy your life.

Chapter One

What are mindsets?

If you've read one of my other books, you'll have read the description below. I include it again here as a brief recap on this essential information before getting into the detail of how you get yourself so frazzled, and how to increase your personal resilience and well-being.

Throughout this book, when I mention 'mindsets', I'm thinking of a specific process your brain uses to filter for information.

Our senses take in a huge deluge of information every second – millions of bits of data flooding in via eyes, ears, nose, etc. The brain would be overwhelmed if it actively tried to process all this information, so it doesn't. It actively makes decisions about what information to process and what information to filter out of our attention. As a result, the larger proportion of data received every second is discarded, or not processed by our conscious mind.

As a consequence of this, we often miss large changes to our visual field and can fail to notice something right in front of our eyes – something that would be obvious to somebody else who knows it's there, knows where to look, or knows it's about to happen.

So, every time I mention mindsets, I'm talking about this process by which you 'set' your mind to filter for information, i.e. the largely unconscious neurological process by which your brain decides what information to pay attention to and what information to filter out or discard.

As yet, it's not very clear what it is that sets your mind in this way, but it's probably a long list of factors: your beliefs, how you were brought up, what you did yesterday, your physical state, how much alcohol you drank last night, how much exercise you've taken recently, and so on. (*For more detail about this topic, check out the legendary work of Simons & Chabris[1], or books by Daniel J Levitin[2], Carol Dweck[3], or Richard Wiseman[4].*)

One of the ways in which your mindsets may manifest themselves is in little unconscious instructions, rules or directions you give yourself – little ways in which you tell yourself to look at things...

one way or another

This book will explore simple but significant possibilities for replacing how you look at things one way with how you *could* look at things another .

Chapter Two

What's on your mind?

This is the crucial chapter – very little of what follows will make good sense if you don't get this bit first, so turn up your attention for a page or two. I'll keep it short and simplify everything massively – if you want to read the technical stuff for yourself, use the bibliography at the end to hunt down the detail.

The bit of your brain behind your forehead is literally the container of what's 'on your mind'. It's the part of your brain called the pre-frontal cortex. This is such a mouthful that, from here on, I'll just call it LittleBrain.

Here he is:

As you can see, he's your personal superhero.

And this is where he lives:

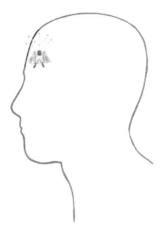

Sometimes we'll call him LB for short.

He has superpowers: *Memorising, Recalling, Understanding, Decision-Making and Inhibiting.*

And he uses these superpowers in different combinations to do great jobs for you at your command, e.g. *prioritising, analysing, interpreting, creative work, deep thought, telling jokes.*

LittleBrain also puts the brakes on – he *stops you (*stops you from thinking about stuff you shouldn't, so that, instead, you can do the stuff you should. This is known as *Inhibiting*).

But LittleBrain is much newer than many other parts of your brain.

And, maybe due to inexperience, compared with other, older and wiser parts of your brain, it takes a lot of energy for LittleBrain to do the stuff you ask.

So, whenever LittleBrain does any of these important things, he uses up a lot of your available mental fuel (glucose).

Your brain doesn't have a fuel tank to maintain a reserve supply of glucose, so…

Once he's started using up this mental fuel, LittleBrain doesn't have enough fuel left to do any more of the important tasks to the same level of performance as he did before – he needs to rest or to refuel.

If LittleBrain hasn't had enough sleep, he'll be tired and, once again, he won't perform.

But he doesn't know how to tell you he's tired or out of fuel (and you're probably not listening anyway), so he slogs on through, doing whatever you task him with.

You take a long while to notice LittleBrain isn't performing as well as he was before – it's a bit like doing stuff after you've drunk some alcohol – you still think you're performing brilliantly (sometimes you might think you're more brilliant than you were before the alcohol – but you're not). It's the same with LittleBrain: you think he's doing fine, when he's not anymore.

And as he gets tired or hungry, LittleBrain does other stuff for you, too – stuff that sometimes you wish he wouldn't. Stuff like *reminding you of things you've forgotten, getting stuck thinking about something you don't want to, worrying about stuff, chatting to you about stuff you ought to be doing instead* ("*Watch TV!*") and so on.

When this starts to happen, when LittleBrain gets distracted (or when you get him distracted) he doesn't cope very well and his performance drops, but you don't notice – or you try not to notice, because you'd rather he stopped moaning and just got on with it.

As he gets tired, he gets a little bored too – he needs something different (not much) to revive him or wake him again – something as simple as looking in a different direction or changing his surroundings. Again, you don't realise – you keep him sitting in the same position, looking in the same direction, staring at the same screen for much too long.

And, of course, the biggest challenge here is that, once LittleBrain needs to rest or refuel, he's no longer very good at Making Decisions, prioritising or stopping you from thinking about things you shouldn't be thinking about.

So, even when you manage to notice he needs to rest or refuel, he's not going to provide you with the decisiveness to make the necessary things happen – he's not going to be decisive about the break or the fuel you need.

Finally, there are several things that LittleBrain just isn't very good at – in truth, he's rubbish at them, but you ask him to do them anyway. He's not very good at consciously trying to pay attention to two different things at once; he's not very good when he tries to do two different mental jobs at the same time, e.g. analyse information and Make Decisions; he's not very good when you ask him to consider too many different pieces of information together, or information that is too complex while you complete other tasks; and he gets tired and badly behaved quite quickly when you ask him to try to hold onto and remember interesting background information while focusing on and actively thinking about specific details.

LittleBrain doesn't like these kinds of activities, because they use up so much fuel and increase the pace at which he's going to become tired.

Despite this, even when he's tired, you insist to yourself, and to your friends and colleagues that you *are* good at these things. You hear yourself saying weird things like:

Poor LittleBrain – even while he's struggling, he has to listen to this nonsense.

And, as if that's not enough to cope with, next you get unreasonable. You ask LittleBrain to do all these things that he's not good at (multi-tasking, analysing and Decision-Making together, doing a piece of work while listening to another conversation, reading an e-mail while listening to a presentation) quickly, or even immediately. Sometimes when you do this, LittleBrain just stops trying or even goes into shock.

So, in summary:

LittleBrain is your personal servant.

He lives in the small space just behind your forehead.

You're very demanding of him.

He doesn't always cope so well.

He gets tired and you don't notice.

He needs rest and you don't give it to him.

He needs food to refuel and you don't give it to him.

He needs enough sleep to recuperate, but you're tempted to do other stuff instead – you want to have fun, after all, to have a life, to feel good (oh, the irony!).

16

He needs novelty and difference to raise his interest and his game, but, instead, you keep him sitting in the same place, looking the same way for much too long.

He stops performing so well and you don't even notice.

He stops working or goes into shock. Still you don't notice – you keep asking him to do more.

This way your mind (LittleBrain) works, this way you make demands of your mind, not noticing or ignoring what it really needs, this is how you get frazzled. There's more involved, much more, but this is the basis.

Much of the rest of what I'll explore in this short book is about specific things that can cause this, specific things that can make this worse and, of course, specific things to do when it's happening, or to lessen the possibility it's going to happen at all.

But essentially, this is the starting point.

Chapter Three

So what?

OK, so what's all this nonsense talk about LittleBrain? Well, remember, we're really talking about the pre-frontal cortex – that bit of your brain behind your forehead. It's literally the bit of your brain that holds 'what's on your mind'. When it gets tired, it stops functioning well and when it gets overloaded, it can't get its act in gear. And when you overload it with too many things at once, too much information, ask it to look and act in two different directions at once, then it just doesn't perform well, and even while it's not performing well, this dual-task interference makes it tired – really tired. Once *it's* not performing, then *you* can't perform – those significant mental tasks become much more difficult, kind of fuzzy and, when you keep going, trying to push through this fuzziness, you encourage the feeling of overload, you start to feel you can't perform, you start to experience stress. If you continue to push on through, your body, your whole nervous system starts to respond and starts to gear up to deal with this continuing state of strain and stress. Over time, constantly trying to push through the fuzziness rather than taking deliberate – often counterintuitive – steps to change your state, can lead to serious stress, anxiety, even burnout.

Of course, what you do to LittleBrain, you do to yourself.

Now, you're going to need to respond to all this news by noticing and playing with the various mindsets available to you.

This sounds too difficult – this book is already a strain on my LittleBrain. I'll stop reading and send a few fun texts instead	vs	If I can just make a few simple changes, I can feel better and start to make things different
I'm not multi-tasking and overloading myself; it's my boss, it's the organisation I work for	vs	Some of this is down to me – I need some new habits; if I'm more disciplined, I can affect some of this

In this book, I'm suggesting the two blue mindsets over here.

To be honest, it *is* going to be tricky, but even just an increased awareness will begin to make a substantial difference – so keep reading and stay with me.

And while there's absolutely no doubt your boss or your organisation will accidentally or deliberately do things that make you mistreat LittleBrain, there are some simple actions that are definitely in your power to take that will improve things substantially (though again, they'll require some effort).

Chapter Four

How this book works

Here's what we'll do.

1   We'll explore a little more what happens to LittleBrain, and how you mistreat him. And then what he does to you, accidentally, in return.

2   At regular intervals, we'll take a quick look at examples of these kinds of actions – changes you might make to your day and week to keep the frazzle at bay.

3   We'll explore a dozen everyday disciplines or activities that can make a significant difference to your well-being and resilience. Most of us are already doing many of these activities regularly through the week. But we'll explore how changing the balance of time and energy you invest in them can help LittleBrain stay more resourceful and fight off the frazzle, leaving you feeling emotionally and mentally stronger and more capable.

4   We'll look at some simple changes you might make to change the balance of these everyday disciplines – small changes that ensure you're spending appropriate time and energy on each one.

So, in summary, this book will help you to:

Realise how you abuse LittleBrain, making him frazzled.

Make small but significant changes to reduce this abuse.

Understand how some everyday activities and disciplines contribute to your bedrock of resilience.

Change the balance of time and energy you invest in these activities and disciplines so you become stronger and more resilient.

You may have spotted already that these elements form a downward spiral when you get them wrong, and a virtuous cycle that feeds itself positively when you get them just right.

Structuring your day: One

There are so many implications for the way we structure our days that we'll have a look at this a few times. On each occasion, we'll consider:

Stuff you shouldn't do and **Stuff you should do instead**

Now, if you're reading this, I expect you're a human, and just because there's stuff you shouldn't do and stuff you should do instead doesn't mean that's what you're going to do, does it? In fact, sometimes, if you *are* a human, you'll quite deliberately do the 'stuff you shouldn't do' *because* you've been told you shouldn't do it.

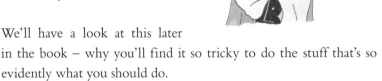

We'll have a look at this later in the book – why you'll find it so tricky to do the stuff that's so evidently what you should do.

For now, I suggest you just start soaking up these straightforward suggestions – and worry about the how-tos and the whether -I-can-dos" later.

What we've covered about LittleBrain already is enough to suggest some changes we should make, and this involves the discipline of Right stuff at the right time.

LittleBrain is at his best when he's got plenty of fuel, when he's fresh, not tired. So...

The stuff you shouldn't do

✗   Don't start your day, when you're fresh and at your peak, by checking your e-mails. You're wasting LittleBrain's peak performance time. And, by the time you've finished checking through your e-mails, you'll have used up quite a bit of mental fuel and won't have as much left to do the important work.

✗   Don't skip lunch because you're too busy, because you're too macho, or because you're just not disciplined enough.

✗   Don't sit in meetings for hours on end.

The stuff you should do instead

✓   Be brave: start your day by completing a major piece of work you have to get done – something that is going to require some heavy mental activity – analysis, creativity, Decision-Making.

or...

✓   Start your day by completing your planning for the day or the week – prioritising. This is really heavy mental activity, because it uses so many of LB's superpowers in quick succession.

✓   By doing either of these things you'll have made valuable use of your available mental fuel on jobs that really need it. With great comfort, you can then get on with the blander and much less strenuous business of looking through your e-mails.

✓   LittleBrain is going to need regular top-ups of fuel – particularly after you've completed challenging or tiring mental activity. You'll need to make sure you pay attention to this – noticing when you've been working him with conscious processing tasks. Little and often is probably safest.

✓   Find ways to get over the macho behaviour of others you might be meeting with. Make sure you take breaks – either to refuel or just for a quick rest.

✖ And when you take a break, don't use it to exhaust LittleBrain further.

✓ Pay attention to what you do with these breaks. There's good evidence that a change is as good as a rest – focusing on something totally different can be as good as doing nothing; however, don't overdo this strategy either – if, during your breaks, you're always doing something that requires conscious mental application, you're continuing to use up your mental fuel and to place the strain on LittleBrain. Over time, you'll both end up in a world of frazzlement.

Chapter Five

A dozen everyday resilience activities and principles

Right Stuff Right Time is one of a dozen activities or disciplines we're going to explore. First off, a dozen is too many, so we'll slot them into four areas, via their approximate functions, as follows:

Reducing the Abuse	Rest & Recuperation
LittleBrain Training	Bedrock Resilience

As the name makes clear, the first of the four comprises everyday activities and principles that will help you to reduce your mistreatment of LittleBrain; the remaining three areas affect your resilience through rest, training or your ability to build and maintain a solid bedrock. These provide the flipside of your frazzlement; they affect your overall personal state. When you get the right balance of these, LittleBrain will cope better with the abuse he gets.

This is how they break down into the dozen or so activities and disciplines:

Reducing the Abuse

Generally speaking, these principles will stop you demanding too much of LittleBrain, overloading him, tiring him, or making him do stuff when he'd rather not. They comprise:

Right Stuff Right Time: not tasking LittleBrain with stuff to do when he doesn't want to, when he's already too tired or when he's hungry. We already started to look at this principle a couple of pages ago and it'll crop up again in several places.

Simplification & Chunking: disciplining yourself to look at complex information, and to communicate it to others in ways that pulls it together into graspable chunks, and makes it as succinct as is possible. This reduces the level of frazzle we're inflicting on LittleBrain. This isn't about dumbing down your information – it's about working out what's really needed and stopping your indulgence in information for the sake of it.

Externalising Thoughts: the ability to get thoughts out of your head, so you don't have to waste LittleBrain's energy continuing to memorise, recall and understand stuff every time you want to do things with that stuff. This includes recording thoughts (e.g. in writing), and turning thoughts into objects, e.g. a calendar, a book, a library, a peg for my car keys (every time I need to think about finding them, I won't have to – they're there). Sounds like another obvious one, but you may not be making as much of this as you could to reduce the frazzle.

Changing State: how your physiology and your movement can affect your state, freshen up LittleBrain or rebalance your brain chemicals so LittleBrain feels different – better even!

Rest & Recuperation

These principles allow LittleBrain to recover by giving him time off, or giving him rest. This enables other parts of your brain to do their work – to integrate, learn and make sense of everything. They comprise:

Sleep: duhhh! Yep, this one's about the amount and quality of sleep you manage to get. Seems obvious, but it's essential, given the major impact it will make on your daily sense of well-being, your stress levels, and your emotional and mental health.

Chilling Out: this discipline is essential for your unconscious ability to make sense of the sensory bombardment you receive on a daily basis; it provides LittleBrain with serious deep recovery time, and allows your nervous system to integrate what you're experiencing and learning so you make sense of the world.

Refuelling: remember, your brain doesn't have a store for glucose, LittleBrain's fuel supply, so you need to make sure your food intake is regular and timed to help his recovery from major work sessions, so he can continue to use his superpowers without frazzling himself.

LittleBrain Training

I've grouped these together because they're all somehow about broadening the types of stress you give LittleBrain – productive stress that helps him increase his superpowers. These comprise:

Attention-Span Development: the quality of your hobbies and pastimes – spare-time activities that enhance your attention span. Get these right, and they're like trips to the gym for LittleBrain: you get to do stuff you really enjoy while he works out. And these workouts help increase his superpowers and reduce the chances of frazzlement.

Fun-Play: the time and energy you put into mucking around, having some fun and literally playing. Time spent in this way is another version of an enjoyable trip to the gym. This discipline promotes emotional intelligence, social learning and your ability to transfer LittleBrain's skills from one scenario to another.

Stopping – Quiet Time: an absence of busy, output-focused thinking. Moments when you create a quiet, calm, non-judgmental focus on your surroundings and your state. These moments give LittleBrain a major break, but, more significantly, they help him learn how to manage the overload of think-think-think through your days and nights.

Bedrock Resilience

These activities are the trend over a longer period of time. When you get them just right, they provide you with a stronger sense of long-term resilience, i.e. they'll affect the state you're already in when you begin to work LittleBrain each day. These comprise:

Exercise: this strengthens your brain's ability to make and sustain neural connections (the basis for learning and mental strength), it increases the presence of brain chemicals that promote better sleep and a sense of well-being, it produces a better balance of brain chemistry, and moderates the effects of the stress chemical, cortisol.

Relationships: the amount of time and energy you manage to put into developing and maintaining strong close relationships for their own sake (rather than time and energy you put into getting jobs and tasks done that happen to involve others, and require you to interact with them). Think of this as the fundamental bedrock of your resilience.

Learning: genuinely learning from a situation, rather than looking at it only as either success or failure, achievement or non-achievement, promotes greater resilience and the ability to cope.

The astute reader will notice I've listed thirteen activities – it's a Baker's Dozen. None of them is out of the ordinary or strange – they're quite normal elements of most peoples' lives – although the balance of time and energy we each manage to spend on them is usually quite different. The point here is to help you to look at the balance *you* are achieving.

This will be a continuous project, where you'll need to keep making adjustments as your sense of frazzlement, resilience and well-being ebbs and flows. So, understanding the implications of each activity, identifying major gaps you have and finding simple ways to address these is highly significant.

My own sense of well-being and resilience has increased significantly via a number of these activities while I've been writing this book – mainly because I've been tougher with myself on some of my more dubious decisions about what I do daily and weekly. It's not taken much attention to enable these changes to occur – it's this productive awareness that I hope you will achieve as you read.

Balance

Consider the balance you believe you're currently achieving. Identify how satisfied you are currently with the time and energy you put into each. Mark each out of 100, where one is as dissatisfied as you could be and 100 suggests you're smug about how well you're doing.

Reducing the Abuse		
	Right Stuff Right Time	%
	Simplification & Chunking	%
	Externalising Thoughts	%
	Changing State	%

Rest & Recuperation	Sleep	%
	Chilling Out	%
	Refuelling	%

LittleBrain Training	Attention-Span Development	%
	Fun-Play	%
	Stopping – Quiet Time	%

Bedrock Resilience	Exercise	%
	Relationships	%
	Learning	%

Chapter Six

Sleep

This is the first of the **Rest & Recuperation** activities. There are a couple of big ideas to take on board regarding sleep. But before we get to them, let's take a quick look at some mindset balances you might need to consider.

With the invention of artificial light, and then the arrival of all kinds of electrical and automatic gadgets designed to complete industrial and domestic jobs for us, our attitude towards sleep has changed significantly.

I notice in others and in myself, the following mindset tensions:

Sleep is a necessity	Sleep is a luxury
Sleep isn't productive	Sleep makes me productive
The longer I stay up the less productive I become	If I stay up longer I can get more done

Sleep isn't fun (so I compromise on it)	Damn right! Breathing's not 'fun' either, but I can't compromise on it, so I don't
Sleep increases my quality of life when I'm awake	If I spend too long in bed, I'm missing out on my life
I don't need much sleep; only the old and the very young need lots of sleep	Too little sleep and I don't feel so young

I hear the pink mindsets above much more than I hear the blue ones. I confess I use the pink ones myself more often than is helpful, and sometimes much more than I've used the blues. Yet, there's a growing awareness of the huge importance of the right amount and quality of sleep in preserving LittleBrain's abilities, in maintaining our resilience and sustaining our sense of well-being.

And while there are still plenty of studies that suggest the amount of sleep we need varies somewhat from individual to individual[5], there are some that conclude the right amount of sleep is increasingly specific: nine hours a night is too much; less than six is too little[6]. So, now, as we look at two big ideas about sleep, just keep an eye on your own prevailing mindsets, and check whether you need to address the balance in your attitude – check whether you need a rethink regarding your self-talk about your sleep.

The stages of sleep
Every night, through the night, when you're asleep, you go through sleep cycles of approximately ninety minutes. Ideally, your sleep time should allow for complete cycles: seven and a half to eight hours allows for four to five complete cycles.

Typically, if you wake before the end of a cycle you'll feel groggy.

Each of these cycles proceeds through five different stages of sleep. And each of these stages has its own particular function for your health and well-being. A very rough idea of this would be:

> Stage 1: relaxing and loosening conscious control.
> Stage 2: physical learning strengthened – the activity you learnt during the day is replayed in order to cement it.
> Stage 3: information is consolidated as knowledge and cognitive learning is replayed.
> Stage 4: repair of damaged tissue, hormones and chemicals is rebalanced.
> Stage 5: dreaming sleep – memories are laid down, traumatic events processed and dealt with and fresh perspectives are generated, both in learning and meaning[7].

> "Even a single night of sleep deprivation can render one more negative and more emotionally unregulated the next day than is experienced with a full night of restorative sleep."
>
> David Rock, Daniel J Siegel, Steven AY Poelmans & Jessica Payne, The Healthy Mind Platter, NeuroLeadership Journal, Issue Four, p5 , October 2012

You can see immediately that, when we muck about with the quality of sleep we get, there are going to be some significant implications. When we don't get enough deep sleep – stages 3 and 4 – we directly risk our resilience and well-being, physically as well as mentally; the overload of information we're experiencing and the learning we're supposed to take from this information may not be consolidated; the following day, our cognitive functioning will be degraded; emotionally we'll be a bit frayed; and our physical health will not be properly restored.

The circadian rhythm

It wasn't until the invention of the mainspring in the fifteenth century that clocks became portable. Even then, the popularity of watches didn't spread through Europe until the sixteenth century, and minute hands didn't appear on them until the late seventeenth century. How in the world did humans know when to go to bed, when to get up?

Animal and plant life has a profound understanding of the daily rhythm of things. Flowers don't open their petals in response to the sun – they open their petals in response to their own internal sense of time. Put them in a dark cupboard and they continue to keep their daily routines of opening and closing. Make humans live underground in a deep cave, with no timekeeper, no access to the world above and no artificial light, and they will continue to maintain their daily routine, waking, eating and sleeping to the same pattern.

This is the circadian rhythm. It's our innate response to the pattern of the day. This internal clock readjusts slightly, depending on levels of light it experiences, so it can respond to the seasons – and even artificial light will cause this slight adjustment.

This internal response to the pattern of the day means our energy, our sense of awakeness or tiredness is not constant across the day. This has big implications for LittleBrain, the way we treat him and how he responds.

Typically, our circadian rhythm goes something like this:

> 6am – 11am Moving from sleepy to awake and alert.
> 11am – 3pm Decreasing alertness.
> 3pm – 4pm Waking-hours low point for alertness and energy (really, your circadian rhythm is prompting you to sleep here).
> 4pm – 8pm Gradual increase to waking-hours high point.
> 9pm – 12am Declining energy and alertness towards sleep[8].

Do a quick search of the internet for circadian rhythm images and you'll come up with all kinds of far out, creative renditions; but I think the simple version by Richard Wiseman, from his book *Night School*[9], really communicates the significance and power of what's going on. I've simplified it further for our purposes here, so take a look at Wiseman's book for more detail.

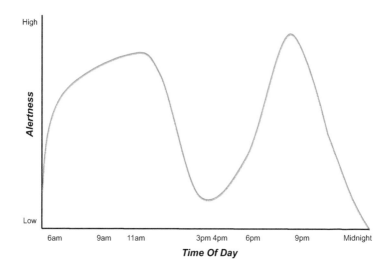

As this is the way our bodies have learnt to behave, starting to muck about with this rhythm too much is going to impact on your health and well-being. For example, even small amounts of light from your television, your phone or from any electrical appliances will be enough to adjust your circadian rhythm, causing a change in your body's understanding of when it should fall asleep[10]. Some studies have found that too much screen time at any time of the day substantially increases your chances of sleep deprivation[11]. So, be careful how much light you expose yourself to, particularly after 9pm, when your nervous system knows it's supposed to be easing down towards sleep. Jet lag is like your nervous system internally knowing it should be asleep while you consciously override this knowledge. You could think of it like your nervous system going into shock while you do this bizarre thing to it.

But the circadian rhythm isn't just about sleep – it's also about reducing the abuse via the principle of Right Stuff Right Time. If you look back at the graph of the rhythm, then clearly there are big implications for when you make the biggest demands on LittleBrain, so you're not working him hard when he really wants to rest or sleep and recover. The first half of the morning and late afternoon into evening immediately look like good time slots for more intense, demanding mental activity, compared to the middle of the afternoon.

Larks and owls

Sadly, it's not always quite as simple as all this. Our individual circadian rhythms can vary on the basis of whether we're broadly more a morning person (lark) or more an evening person (owl). Unless you're an extreme of one of these, it's likely this will mean your own circadian rhythm would naturally be slightly earlier or later than the above timings, maybe as much as an hour or more. If you know you're quite strongly an evening person, then it'll be helpful to realise your peaks and troughs of energy and attention will be a while later than pictured above. Morning or evening, you'll need to account for this in the suggestions and instructions I've listed in this chapter.

But don't overdo it. Even if you are more one or the other, bear in mind that if your working hours are something conventional, like 8.30am to 6pm, then you're already making adjustments to your circadian rhythm by exposing yourself to light in line with these working hours, and this helps you function. If you're an evening person, but you need to be up and on it early each day, then do what you can to bombard yourself with light early, and keep it up through the morning as much as you can. This will help adjust your rhythm in line with your working hours. It won't help to let this drift over the weekend – stay on it during days off, if you can.

Structuring your day: Two

LittleBrain needs sleep in order to process learning and information and in order to recover and regain a balanced perspective. So…

Stuff you shouldn't do

✗　Don't muck about with your circadian rhythm too regularly or too much.

✗　Don't habitually work on into the night – past 8pm. Too much light or mental tasking after this time may disrupt your sleep pattern.

✗　Don't burn the candle at both ends – partying hard too regularly – and still expect the same performance standards from LittleBrain – your learning capacity, cognitive ability, logical reasoning and emotional state will all be affected by less sleep.

Stuff you should do instead

✓　Allow yourself to ease down towards sleep after 9pm, reducing the amount of light and strenuous mental activity. Stop using your light-producing electrical gadgets in good time before you want to sleep.

✓　Be prepared for the impact that partying has on your cognitive ability the next day. Plan your diary so you're not in heavyweight thinking sessions or required to complete taxing mental work when you're going to be sleep-deprived.

✓　Check your party schedule – be careful how much partying you plan into a week or month. It won't only affect your ability to work – too much will create a downward spiral towards a more serious state of frazzlement (what a killjoy LittleBrain is!).

Owing to your circadian rhythm, LittleBrain is naturally tired at particular times, so your conscious cognitive mental ability will be quite different at certain times of the day.

✗　Don't do the wrong type of work at the wrong time for LittleBrain.

✗　Don't leave your important, mentally demanding tasks for mid-afternoon.

✓　Make the best of your freshness. The circadian rhythm suggests early to mid-morning and early evenings will get the best performance from LittleBrain and his key functions (so long as you haven't thrashed him or starved him too much by then). Schedule key creative, analytical, Decision-Making work for these times.

✘ Don't stay awake between 3 and 4pm.

✓ Just joking – I'm trying to help your sense of well-being, and losing your job won't do this.

✓ Actually, there are workplaces where it has become in vogue to put your head on your desk and take a nap. There are studies that demonstrate how beneficial for LittleBrain napping can be, the varied benefits of different lengths of naps[12] and how it's slightly better to nap in bed than at your desk[13]. But far be it from me to make such recommendations, when I haven't tried it myself.

✘ Don't ever – not ever – find yourself in a mentally demanding meeting at 3.30 in the afternoon.

✓ Yes, I know this one's unrealistic as well, but see what you can do. And when you do find yourself in a meeting between 3 and 4pm, be ready, be prepared, be brave if needed:

✓ Have a light snack before you begin – nuts, fruit, rice crackers – to increase the fuel available for LittleBrain during this challenging time. Don't eat much, though – you'll make things worse.

✓ During the meeting, change the place you sit – move to a different chair (a couple of times) – even the smallest amount of novelty will help to arouse LittleBrain.

✓ Or don't sit at all during these meetings – standing may help to increase LittleBrain's oxygen levels to help him through the lull.

✓ Ask for a couple of breaks.

✓ Stick your head out of the window during these breaks and get some fresh air to LittleBrain.

✓ Go for a stroll, if you can.

✓ Make sure you drink some water – again, see if you can increase his oxygen supply.

✓ Picture a problem or something going wrong. This helps to arouse LittleBrain.

✓ Resist the urge to cram in more cognitive work during these breaks (don't catch up on your e-mails or continue to debate a point with one of your colleagues during your stroll).

Of course, these 'things you should do' don't just apply to meetings you're in between 3 and 4pm; they apply to any meetings – helping to reduce the strain on LittleBrain throughout the day will increase your resilience and resourcefulness over the long term.

10 things to try to get a better night's sleep

1   Squeeze more physical exercise into your day. Even a brisk walk during the day will increase your levels of serotonin – a calming, feel-good, helpful-for-sleep brain chemical.

> "Despite claims to the contrary, no one is impervious to the stimulant effects of caffeine. Some people insist that they can drink strong coffee in the evening without affecting their sleep. But the reason why they can still fall asleep is not because their bodies are miraculously immune to the pharmacological actions of caffeine: it is because their sleepiness is sufficiently strong to overwhelm the stimulant effect."
>
> Paul Martin, *Counting Sheep*, p147

2   Work out how much caffeine is useful for you, and where the limit is. I still appear to be able to sleep well on two caffeinated coffees as long as I drink them in the morning, but if I go beyond two, and particularly if I have one after lunch, things don't go so well when I get to bed at night. This is probably because, for most of us, caffeine levels in our bodies halve every six hours. So, if I drink a coffee at midday, by 6pm half the caffeine from that cup is still circulating in my body[14]. The equally important point here is not about the caffeine itself – it's about making sure you're tired

enough to sleep. This is one of the reasons we need to balance these everyday activities. If you don't achieve this balance:

    a) You'll frazzle LittleBrain and yourself by overdoing very narrow and specific kinds of stress (multi-tasking, continuous partial attention, lack of recuperation or rest for LittleBrain, lack of time off for LittleBrain).

    b) You won't actually stress LittleBrain in enough different, broader ways – ways that build his strength and capability differently, ways that help tire you out so you sleep, without keeping him stuck in the frazzlement of narrow-task work focus, e.g. Exercise, Attention-Span Development and Fun-Play will help tire him enough for sleep.

3   Develop a strong bedtime routine that gets you into a state for sleep – notice the sequence of things you do that are best at getting you into sleepiness:

> Evening meal
>   Hobby time
>   Chat with my partner
>   Watch TV
>   Play a game
>   Warm bath
>   Read something fun
>   Snuggle down

This is just an example – and a ridiculously packed example it is. Take a look and identify which of these induces sleepiness in you. I've noticed the best last thing in my sequence is some reading – though I must make sure it's easy reading. By contrast, going from watching TV straight to trying to sleep just doesn't work for me (of course).

4   Notice when you're yawning and ready for bed – stop what you're doing and get yourself tucked up. Recently, I've noticed that if I'm watching a programme on TV in the evening, I'll

naturally get to a point where I start to nod. I'm so determined that I'm watching TV, I'll stay sitting there, nodding and waking, nodding and waking. Ironically, once the programme's finished and I go to bed, it's like I've missed the moment – I get into bed and feel wide awake. Get to bed when you're ready.

5   Keep a notebook and pen by your bed – this is a technique from the discipline of Externalising Thoughts. If you wake up thinking about things, write them down as quickly as possible – the quicker they're on the page, the sooner they're out of your head (literally moving them out of LittleBrain and onto the page), the sooner you can get back to sleep.

6   Stop stimulating LittleBrain with too much information, light and energy until really late, then still expect to fall asleep straightaway. As I was writing this, a friend of mine explained that, because she's so busy all day, when she falls into bed at night, she reviews her task list for the next day, then gets her tablet out and checks the day's posts on social-media sites, some of them work-related. Ironically, she hadn't really thought properly that this might be the reason she doesn't get to sleep easily or wakes up in the middle of the night with LittleBrain whirring and talking to her about her work.

7   It's a long-established fact that your body cools down in readiness for sleep, so bedtime routines that encourage this can be useful, e.g. this is why a warm bath before bed can work well. Make sure the water isn't too hot (if it is, you won't cool quickly enough) and take the bath a little before bedtime, so you're ready to jump into bed once your body is cooling off nicely.

8   Lessen your intake of alcohol: when we start to feel frazzled, some of us reach for alcohol as a convenient and fast way to feel relaxed. That seems to make sense, but the alcohol works more systematically to muck about with our essential Rest & Recuperation. While it may help you to fall asleep more easily, it will then affect the quality of your sleep – you may not experience enough of the deeper stages. So, while you may

dream a lot, consolidation, repair and emotional balancing may not occur fully. In this way, over a period of time, alcohol could increase any feelings of stress you may have – you believe it's easing the frazzlement, but it could actually be making it worse! Darn it!

9   Create a good sleep environment. The key features to focus on are:
- darkness (block out the light as much as possible, for reasons discussed above).
- safety/security/quiet – your unconscious will stay on alert through the night for disturbances and safety issues, so knowing this is taken care of will be helpful[15].

As you've been reading the above list about less alcohol, less late-night phone use, less TV-watching in bed, less caffeine, more exercise, more discipline, you may have noticed a couple of mindsets starting to creep into your thinking:

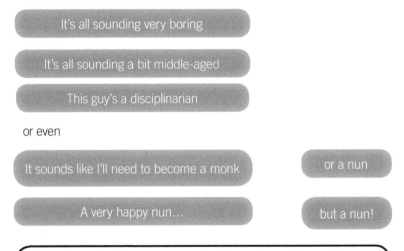

It's all sounding very boring

It's all sounding a bit middle-aged

This guy's a disciplinarian

or even

It sounds like I'll need to become a monk   or a nun

A very happy nun...   but a nun!

> **WARNING**
> With all of the dozen disciplines we're going to look at in this book, it's very easy to become overly serious, a bit of a bore, a lecturing-evangelical-know-it-all-who-can't-resist-preaching-about-the-best-way-to-behave-to-everyone-they-meet.

This isn't the point of this book! If you rigidly, and very seriously follow the disciplines here – all of them, to the letter – you'll get very tense, you're likely to become inflexible, you'll possibly become insufferable to those around you. This tension will decrease your well-being significantly, and possibly the well-being of your colleagues and loved ones too.

This whole idea is about balance – continuing to seek a good balance, a better balance for your situation right now. What works well for some months may stop working so well when your situation changes slightly around you, so becoming too rigid about it all isn't helpful. Don't make discipline into an obsession! Obsession is not well-being.

Which brings us to…

10   Take it easy. Once you're aware you want more quality sleep, it's tempting to get tense about what's going on; it's tempting to try too hard; it's tempting to get uptight when other people around you don't follow the same routine as you ("You're disturbing my routine!"). Don't try so hard that you get stressed about it. Do enough, but relax. Try making small adjustments, one thing at a time ("I'll just stop checking my e-mails and social media after 9pm at night, and during this time, I'll watch a bit of TV then I'll read a book instead.") This might be enough to do the job.

Which leads us to the possibility of:

11   Break all the rules; try doing everything wrong for a couple of nights. It's likely the rebellion, the fun, the relaxation involved and the build-up of tiredness will result in the restoration of good sleep. Remember, good sleep is a habit – you're more likely to sleep well when you get into the habit, so, similarly, if you're in the habit of following a set of sleep 'procedures' that aren't working (even if they *are* remorselessly sensible), break the habit.

Chapter Seven

Under the influence

While your well-being and your state are related to the state of LittleBrain, they're also influenced more generally by the chemical balance your brain is experiencing. Neurotransmitters are a group of chemicals that are used directly in the process by which information, instructions, signals and responses move through networks in the brain. They're an essential part of the medium by which your brain works effectively.

Changing State, Exercise and Relationships affect the balance of chemicals in your brain both moment by moment, and over a long period. The positive chemical alterations they produce affect your resilience.

I'll mention such shifts in the balance of neurochemicals as we go, but to give some first indications of what we're talking about, here are a few examples:

Relationships and the level of social support you create around you alter the balance of neurotransmitters in favour of oxytocin and serotonin – these are sometimes referred to as the 'feel-good' chemical[16] and the 'leadership' chemical respectively[17]. So, moments in which you actively develop and maintain your high-quality, close relationships will give you an oxytocin buzz of belonging, safety, and feel-goodness; and those moments when you actively reinforce these high-quality, close relationships can give you a serotonin buzz of mutual respect, pride in each other and in yourself. Serotonin "has a calming effect that helps us to assure ourselves that we are going to survive and elevates mood and self-esteem[18]." So, its effects and benefits reach across a number of different areas of life, e.g. its presence can counteract anxiety and fear, but its calming effects mean it's also good for sleep.

Changing the place you're sitting in a meeting will fire increases in dopamine – the brain chemical of interest, novelty, attention and reward. Something as apparently insignificant as this positively affects your personal productivity, will have major benefits for your learning and, of course, will produce an upward spiral of a sense of personal capability and achievement, firing further dopamine along the way.

There is an emerging field of research into the way in which exercise affects neurotransmitters.

1   It's clear exercise releases endorphins – chemicals specifically designed to lessen our experience of physical pain.

2   There's growing interest in the possibility that exercise will 'burn off' cortisol, the naturally occurring stress neurotransmitter which our nervous systems produce to get us ready for fight-or-flight responses[19].

3   There is even evidence that exercise encourages the production of brain proteins that may strengthen the structure of the brain itself and increase the growth of connections between brain cells[20].

And so on. I hope you get the idea. There's plenty of reading available that describes all the neuroscience in relation to the material I'm covering in this book. It's much more complete and much better written than I could manage, so I'll try not to go into too much detail about it from here on. Once again, check the bibliography at the end if you want to know more.

Chapter Eight

Relationships

Relationships are very important to us; they give us a sense of purpose, a sense of meaning, a place in the world; they promote in us feelings of safety and security. There is increasing evidence of how central they are to our sense of well-being.

And yet, in talking to people, I often find that genuine relationship development and maintenance is something we neglect – not deliberately or wilfully, but as something which can wait in the queue behind everything else. Here are a few mindsets I hear from people I coach (and from myself from time to time).

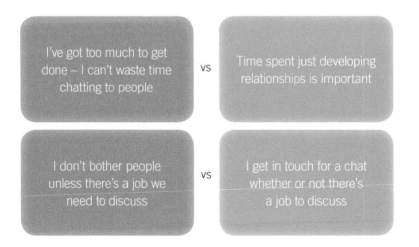

I've got too much to get done – I can't waste time chatting to people

vs

Time spent just developing relationships is important

I don't bother people unless there's a job we need to discuss

vs

I get in touch for a chat whether or not there's a job to discuss

I'm a private person – I keep myself to myself	vs	A problem shared is a problem halved
Watching TV with my partner, together on the sofa, builds our relationship, so we do it a lot	vs	To build our relationship, we need to look at each other, talk to each other, focus on something together
I don't have time for my friends at the moment	vs	I need my friends – they improve my sense of perspective
I have to listen and be polite to people at work all day – I don't have the energy or patience left for yet more of this at home	vs	I need to develop my ability to listen and be patient with the people who matter most – those who form my bedrock of safety & security
You must be joking! My family and friends are the ones who cause me the most grief – I'd rather minimise my time with them	vs	Maybe I need to invest better in these relationships so they're more positive and cause me less stress
I just wish my family could realise how tired I am, and not be so demanding when I get home	vs	I need to do something positive, so I can cope with them and invest positively in them when I get home

Quality relationships are important to the performance of LittleBrain, and affect your well-being in a number of significant ways.

There is no doubt talking to and connecting with people who care about us has positive effects on our levels of stress.

Even things as simple as shaking hands, smiling at someone, being smiled at by someone, helping someone, or being helped by someone increases the brain's levels of oxytocin – the feel-good chemical of social connection and belonging[21]. And this social feel-good factor will balance and moderate levels of cortisol – the natural stress neurochemical that promotes readiness, alertness and the resulting tensions such as raised blood pressure, etc.

There is evidence that the presence of strong social support and caring relationships around an individual will moderate their blood pressure, anxiety and stress; that it also makes people more flexible in their ability to confront psychological challenges and increases their propensity to trust and form further relationships (i.e. it improves our emotional intelligence).[22]

So, the sense that "someone's got my back" (lots of someones – the more the better) has physiological and neurological benefits, and provides us with a lot of social learning.

For some of us, building and maintaining relationships isn't a 'discipline' or an 'activity' – it's just what happens naturally all the time. But not for all of us – some of us need to pay attention and make sure this happens; otherwise, our busy-ness and task focus, our frazzlement and end-of-day tiredness can take over and leave us with less of a social life, less of a significant support network of friends and loved ones.

Certainly it's the case that, after a long and tiring day at work – wading through tasks, talking things through with others – by the time we get back to our nearest and dearest, we feel we've used up all our energy and don't have any left to listen properly, talk to each other, focus on something important together, play with each other.

Neurologically, this *is* the case. Poor LittleBrain – after a long day of intense mental activity at work, he is completely depleted of fuel and in need of a rest.

The big irony is that, while LittleBrain's end-of-day exhaustion may prevent you from investing properly in social relationships, over the long term, he will recover better if you invest in strong long-term relationships.

While it may be evident that we ought to take some positive steps to increase the energy we invest in our relationships, this really is very difficult. Remember, when LittleBrain is exhausted, his performance in the significant mental work we task him with decreases. Given that Decision-Making is one of the key mental activities we task him with, when he's tired, arriving home at the end of the day, he's not going to be capable enough to help you make good decisions about what you ought to do and how to do it. Inhibiting (or stopping your automatic responses, habits and urges) is another of his key functions, so he's not going to fight off your habits and urges very well.

So, if you've abused LittleBrain throughout the day and you get home in a state of frazzlement, it's perfectly understandable that you will be too reactive, responding in a grumpy, snappy or aggressive manner to perfectly reasonable requests for you to listen and pay attention. It's perfectly understandable that, rather than invest in quality human interaction, instead, you growl at people to leave you alone, let you 'chill out' and "be quiet – I can't hear the TV." And while you do this, it's perfectly understandable that you find you can't resist habitual urges to collapse on the sofa, watch undemanding TV, drink a glass of wine and eat something less healthy than you might choose at other times.

Unfortunately, once you've had that glass of wine to help you 'recover,' you've rendered LB even less capable of good Decision-Making, Inhibiting, prioritising and so on.

The big challenge is to realise you can do something about all this. And this really *is* a big challenge, because LittleBrain isn't naturally going to want to do the tasks required to make things different. Not at this point, anyway – he's too tired! (and he might be a little bit confused by alcohol, if you take it on board too quickly).

Of course, LittleBrain's exhaustion is your exhaustion. It's his resulting need for rest that's edging you towards the sofa and the hypnotic mindlessness of easy-going TV: you're both trying to recover from the onslaught of the day. But when you try to recover, standing in front of those who provide your bedrock of security, stability and resilience, you're in danger of trying to recover at their expense.

All of these thoughts aren't naturally going to happen as you arrive home (it's the last thing that will be on your mind). Unless, of course, you develop the intention to have it on your mind. In a funny kind of way, if you can develop the intention to notice all this happening, and if you can actually turn this noticing into a routine, doing it often enough in a week (maybe as few as three times will be enough), then an entirely different part of the brain will be tempted to take over responsibility – a part of the brain that needs less energy to do its job.

So, if you can train yourself to notice these moments as they're happening, and to have a few mindset balances available, you'll be in a position to do something different. Here are a few possibilities. With these mindsets, it's not about choosing one or the other; it's about acknowledging that both are true.

Work has tired me out	and	Some of this is my fault as well – I've misused LittleBrain today
I don't want my evening to tire me further	and	I want a quality evening that will make a positive difference to my week
I need time to recover	and	I need to pick the right time and the right way to recover
I need time to recover	and	I need to take responsibility for my recovery
I need time to recover	and	I need to take deliberate steps to drive my recovery
I need time to recover	and	Maybe I should drive my recovery **before** I get home

If, when you arrive home in your state of frazzlement, you can make it as far as the above mindset balances, then you'll be able to consider a number of ways in which you can change the future.

Change the future?! What!?

Yep! Change the future. Change the evening and the next few days you're about to have. Intervene in the gently downward-sloping spiral of your week.

Structuring your day: Three

A strong circle of good, meaningful relationships will provide a solid bedrock for your Well-Being and Resilience. It will have positive impacts on your physiological and neurological state, which will mean you can cope better.

Stuff you shouldn't do

✗ Don't leave your connection with loved ones solely to chance; spontaneity is great, but it's not the only way to do things.

✗ Don't neglect your partner's well-being in this matter. Your relationship is a system, and in this system, their ability to cope will directly affect your ability to cope. If they're not coping, they'll accidentally give you grief, you'll respond, and off you go in a cycle of heightened cortisol (the stress chemical) and lowered oxytocin (the social feel-good chemical).

Stuff you should do instead

✓ Make plans to meet friends each month, if not each week.

✓ Agree specific times to spend with your loved ones.

✓ Get these plans into your diary, digital calendar or personal organiser – realise they are as important as meetings you have at work, so treat them this way.

✓ Once they're visible in this manner, pay attention to times when they're not regular enough – and plan something in.

✓ Notice if you're thinking "these are my important relationships, and this feels too much like work!". Realise that you might actually need to treat it like a piece of work in order to make it happen.

✓ Make sure you're helping your partner to plan in their regular social time as well – and give them practical assistance to make this possible and achievable.

If you've abused poor LB all day, when you get home, he'll be urging you to rest and recover, rather than invest in close relationships. Ironically, his healthy functioning and your own sense of well-being and resilience relies on these close relationships being strong, well developed and well maintained.

Stuff you shouldn't do

✘ During your journey home, don't work all the way – you've abused poor LittleBrain so much already today, so don't tip him over the edge now. If you do, you should be aware that it's you who's created the exhausted state in which you arrive home – it's you creating the state that means you can't cope with positive human interaction when you arrive in the bedrock of your resilience and well-being.

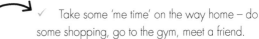

✘ Don't always do this, and, if you do it regularly, don't overdo the time you take on it – this won't help you maintain good relationships at home either.

✘ Don't assume the pub is a good way to do this – you'll arrive home even less capable and decisive.

Stuff you should do instead

✔ Give LittleBrain a well-deserved rest for at least some of the journey home, e.g.:

✔ Take some chill out time to allow him to reflect and incubate without your conscious attention – listen to something undemanding on the radio.

✔ Connect with someone to maintain and develop those important relationships, e.g. on the phone. But consider who it should be – this isn't the time for demanding mental activity, so the people you choose at these moments should be those you can have a laugh and talk rubbish with. Don't pick this as the moment to give your energy and attention to that friend who needs you to listen to their problems and anxieties. If you think this sounds manipulative, consider that if you're to be there for your friends who need your support in this manner, then you're going to need to be in a good state, so that they get good support, empathy and listening from you, rather than poor support and useless listening. Don't do it in a state of frazzlement. Be a bit selfish – the journey home is a time to ease yourself out of frazzlement, rather than increase it.

✔ Take some 'me time' on the way home – do some shopping, go to the gym, meet a friend.

✖ Stop assuming that when you arrive home, you can just walk into the house and be in a great state with those who are there.

✓ Complete a 'Pre-Check'. This one will sound a bit mad, but in our experience, it's the one that makes the biggest difference. You might have read about it in one of our other books, such as *Kill the Robot*. Take a look at how it could work in this context:

- A Pre-Check is a little habit to get into before completing any piece of communication. It's a few moments in which you do some deliberate thinking about yourself:

  – What do I want in this situation?

  – What are my mindsets about it, and about the people involved?

  – What might be more helpful mindsets?

  – How do I want to behave in this situation? What do I want to say and how do I want to say it? What will I make sure I don't say?

- A 'Pre-Check' is a tricky thing to actually do because task focus and busy-ness mean that, usually, I'd prefer to get into the communication, rather than sort myself out ready for the communication.

- It's tricky enough to do this at work, but, significantly, we don't even consider it as important to do when we get home. Here's how it would work:

- If you've driven home, once you arrive, switch off the radio or finish your phone call and stay sitting in your car for a moment or two.

  – Take a few deep breaths in and out.

  – Think about the kind of evening you want – in order to maintain and develop your relationships as the bedrock of your personal resilience.

- Think about your state, e.g. are you too jumpy, too full-on, too angry? Or are you too exhausted – too ready to lie on the sofa and snooze?

- Consider the Pre-Check questions listed above. Wait until you're really ready before you go in.

- Now, of course, when you finally arrive home after a journey, short or long, stopping for a couple of moments of quiet thinking like this will not seem the right thing to do. You won't want to do it (believe me). And, in addition, even if you've chilled out on the way home, or relaxed with some me time or relationship time, LittleBrain may still be too tired to be decisive about the need to do this.

- Think of discipline as your ability to make something happen when you don't want it to happen.

- At first, this will take some tough mental strength, but as I've said before, if you can make it into a routine, then a different part of your brain (the basal ganglia) will be tempted to do it for you – and this won't need or take so much mental fuel.

Yes, I know this is all sounding too much like hard work. I did warn you at the beginning. It's no surprise that so many of us are complaining so regularly about being frazzled, feeling stressed or overwhelmed by it all. The way we're engaging with life/work/play at this point in our history, is particularly ambitious and challenging, but, of course, most of the time we're busy just getting on with it, so we consider it as 'just what we do' – it's normal. So, we fail to realise how demanding and ambitious we're being with ourselves and our little friend LB, who's really quite young as yet, and still has some evolving to do to cope with all of our demands.

Chapter Nine

Stopping – quiet time

Three situations:

1   My train leaves at 6.45 in the morning. I arrive on the platform
    at 6.25. It's a lovely fresh, sunny morning. The birds are
    twittering; the sky is clear. I sit down on a bench. "What shall
    I do?" It's barely a thought, but it's there. I get my phone from
    my pocket, and check my e-mails – no new ones since I left the
    house at 5.45. I think, "Just chill out – have some quiet time."
    I put my phone away. I look around at the birds and the sky.
    I look at the people on the platform opposite. Suddenly I find
    my phone's back in my hand; I'm checking my e-mails – no new
    ones since I left the house at 5.45. I look around at the birds and
    the sky. I breathe in deeply. I get my diary out of my bag,
    and look at my schedule for the day, and the remainder of the
    week. I put my diary away, I look at my phone and check my
    e-mails – a new one! It's spam. I put my phone away. I think,
    "Just chill out – have some quiet time." My train arrives, I board,
    turn on my laptop and get on with my work.

2   I'm in a coffee shop, waiting for a friend to arrive. I look
    around at the other customers. Nobody else is sitting alone.
    I get my phone out of my pocket and check my e-mails (I'll
    look less alone this way). I have two or three e-mails, which
    I deal with in a minute or two. A couple of texts arrive, and
    I respond. I look around at the other customers and the staff
    serving coffee. I consider again how I must look – sitting here

by myself without any friends. I look at my phone – nothing new. I get my diary out, pick up my pen and have a good look at this month's schedule. Now I feel purposeful – now I don't feel I look like such a sad muppet. I check my phone – no new texts, no new e-mails. My friend is late by a minute or two. I look at my phone – maybe they've texted – nothing!

3   My wife and I are walking the dog out in the countryside. The dog runs off up a path – we're not going that way. My wife goes to see where he's got to. I stand and lean on a gate, looking into a meadow of wild flowers. I look at the flowers, I watch the birds and insects flying. She's not back yet – taking longer than I expected. My phone is in my hand before I've thought about it. No texts, no e-mails. I give myself a stern talking to: "You're just standing here for a minute – just do nothing and enjoy the countryside." I put my phone in my pocket, and look around again. I breathe deeply and try to get a hold of myself. "This is mad!" I say to myself. "There's no one around and there's nothing you need to do. You're always hoping for some quiet time – now you've got it, why don't you enjoy it?" My wife and the dog arrive and we continue with our walk.

Mindfulness and meditation are particularly fashionable at the time of writing – they are frequently being used in conversation as a synonym for well-being. Of course, as we're already exploring, there are many more parts of the jigsaw of well-being and resilience than this discipline for Quiet Time; nevertheless, it's a significant contributor in all manner of ways.

One of the reasons it *is* so popular at the moment is there is an increasing need in so many of us to have the skill to stop the flood of internal stimulus – the think-think-think – and take a quiet moment. Many people I coach are reporting very similar experiences to those I've described above in my three scenarios: an inability to stop.

If you're not currently practising a discipline for Quiet Time, then some particular mindsets might kick in the minute words like mindfulness or meditation are mentioned:

This stuff's for hippies

I don't know how to do it – I'd need some training

It's just another 'thing' – if we needed it we'd be doing it already

It's not needed – it's just the latest fad – why can't I sit quietly under a tree instead?

Compare these with some alternatives:

It's only being quiet – it's not some weird or way-out thing

Training would help, but I could just start with some time being quiet

We've been doing it for thousands of years – but I need to reinstate it in myself

I'll just sit quietly under a tree

Mindfulness and meditation are just two specific methods of practising a particular human 'state' – the state of Quiet Time. It's not the same as Chilling Out, when mentally we let it all hang out and follow whatever bit of stimulation or fun we fancy. Instead, it's highly disciplined and requires us to resist the temptation to follow whatever bit of stimulus we fancy and allow ourselves a focus on quiet reflection and an absence of busy thinking. The most thinking we'll do is some calm, considered about-ourselves-and-our-state thinking.

What's important about giving you and LittleBrain enough Quiet Time, is not the discipline you choose to adopt to practise it (e.g. Mindfulness) although many will argue that one discipline is much better than others; what's important, is whether you manage to do it enough, or at all. And whether the method you choose does actually deliver quiet, focused, calm reflection about yourself (rather than just letting it all go or accidentally delivering yet more active stimulus to LittleBrain via busy-thinking or worrying).

Poor LittleBrain – remember how overloaded he is by all the conscious think-think-think all the time? And, it's not just the independent think-think-think that LittleBrain comes up with by himself; it's the addiction to minute-by-minute stimulus we have – and the continuous think-think-think this generates.

- We sit in a coffee shop or on the station platform, phone in hand, and, in seconds, we're swimming in a vast ocean of sound bites and detail, which stimulates more internal thought. This isn't the same as passively watching rubbish TV, which we simply 'receive' without it necessarily generating any internal thought.
- We sit in a coffee shop, or a pub, and there's a huge TV on the wall – and it's constantly switched on (even if the sound is down). And it's tuned to the twenty-four-hour news channel! Again, this is far from the active switching-off of data consumption that would give the Quiet Time that would help.
- We sit at home, apparently relaxing, while we do it to ourselves – we think-think-think about all the things we have to do, planning out our day or week, running through our mental lists of wants-needs-desires-dreams-gripes, worrying about *stuff*.

In the early twenty-first century, it's a constant challenge to stop the active stimulation of LittleBrain – to stop feeding him internal or external stimulus that, in turn, will generate further internal think-think-think.

Here are a number of things that can be done in a way designed to promote genuine Quiet Time. Some of them are actually mindfulness without the label. Some of them are close to meditation, without that label. Some of them are just good ways to do Quiet Time:

- Tai chi.
- The Alexander technique.
- Autogenic training.
- Hypnotherapy.
- Listening to a piece of quiet reflective music, keeping your attention on the different instruments, the different sounds.
- Sitting under a tree, looking and listening to the sights and sounds of nature, again, focusing your attention on and consciously enjoying these sights and sounds, rather than thinking about all kinds of other stuff while you sit there.
- Sitting in a coffee shop looking around at the staff working, at people meeting, just enjoying what they're doing – enjoying the way they're working and the way they're interacting – stopping your critical thinking – stopping your consideration and analysis of whether they're doing a good job or not, whether they're attractive, whether they're your kind of people, whether they're fashionable enough – stopping the judgments you're prone to making about everyone. Allowing yourself to enjoy them doing their thing for a few moments.
- Sitting or standing alone, switching off your phone and other devices and thinking about yourself for a few minutes.
- Going for a walk by yourself for a few minutes and focusing solely on the walk, your surroundings and the action of walking.

- Sitting with your pet dog or cat or budgerigar, watching and listening to them, maybe stroking them and enjoying them being with you – focusing on them, rather than all the things you 'should' be thinking about today.

Some of these things are easier than others; some of them (like the focusing on your pet) can happen quite naturally without you realising you're doing it. The trick is to *notice* you're doing it, and continue to do it without disturbing the calm, considered energy and focus of it.

There. Now you're practising Stopping – Quiet Time.

But what's the point? What am I doing it for?

It's bogus! I'm not actually doing anything!

I just don't have time for this.

Again, at the time of writing, the claims for the benefits of Quiet Time are huge in number and still growing. I'm not sure exactly how many of these are proven scientifically, but here are a few:

- Greater skill in sustained attention[23].
- Greater accuracy in completion of tasks[24].
- Increased capacity of working memory – and therefore short-term reasoning and comprehension[25].
- Increased ability to resist urges and impulses (LittleBrain's super-power of Inhibiting) – i.e. increased emotional well-being[26].
- As a result, there are claims for its ability as a treatment for eating disorders, substance abuse, psoriasis, recurrent depression and chronic pain[27].

- Reduction in cognitive effort required to stay focused (developing LittleBrain's superpowers)[28].

Whether or not all these are shown to be true; we already know LittleBrain is prone to tiredness, exhaustion and frazzlement when we work him too hard, when we don't refuel him or when he becomes tired or confused. We know how difficult he finds it to switch off and inhibit your worries and your think-think-think. We know how too much of this quickly exhausts him, leaving him and you feeling frazzled. So, giving him LittleBrain Training in Stopping – Quiet Time has obvious benefits anyway.

Any of the above ways of 'doing' Quiet Time involves directing the attention of your thoughts in such a way that they take on a calm, focused energy. As I've already said, it's very different from Chilling Out, where you're more likely to have an absence of deliberate, conscious thinking at all. The idea of Quiet Time is that you're still working LittleBrain, but you're working him in a very particular way – you're consciously building his ability to *inhibit* too much think-think-think. It's non-thinking thinking. If you're using one of the approaches that includes paying close attention to real-world sensory data – focusing on the sights and sounds of nature, or paying attention to the feeling of stroking your pet dog or cat or budgerigar (really, do people do this?!), you're learning to switch your mental fuel supply away from LittleBrain and into other parts of your brain, e.g. your visual cortex, your auditory cortex, your motor cortex. This fuel switch gives LittleBrain a rest – time out from full-on think-think-think. Not only are you training him to develop his Inhibiting power, you're giving him a break from over-exertion.

The more skilled you and LittleBrain become at this bizarre skill of 'conscious-thinking-in-a-way-where-you're-doing-less-thinking', the more you'll be able to do it whenever you wish, wherever you wish.

This is quite something. It's like increasing LittleBrain's superpowers. Now he's more capable of defeating the evil Dr Overwhelm, the nefarious Professor Continuous Partial Attention, and the terrible Madame Dual-Task Interference.

After skilful Stopping – Quiet Time, people feel refreshed. This makes sense, because Quiet Time gives LB some time to focus without the demand for him to Memorise, Recall, Understand and Make Decisions. At the most, you're tasking him to do one thing (Inhibiting – stopping other thoughts, urges or distractions from taking your attention); you're not tasking him to think too quickly, to process too much information or to analyse or be creative. So, when you successfully Stop and have Quiet Time, you're giving him a very clear and simple brief that doesn't take so much energy and allows him to feel supremely capable.

Let's get back to some of the tricky mindsets we need to deal with:

> I don't know how to do it – I'd need some training

> Training would help, but I could just start with some time being quiet

While writing this chapter, over the past few weeks, I've remembered my own big challenge about Quiet Time.

> The first challenge is to stop

For some time, I considered I didn't know how to do mindfulness and meditation, and this provided me with a convenient thinking loop, as follows:

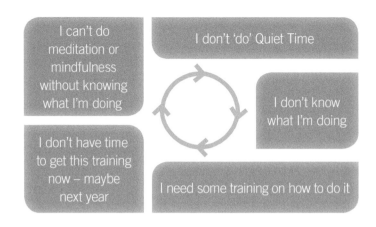

What a freakish thinking trap to get myself into! Luckily, I talk to enough people to know I'm not alone in this kind of self-defeating behaviour – it's perfectly normal (if not helpful).

If you're anything like me, and you recognise some of the twitchy, can't-keep-still, must-be-doing-something behaviours I've described (e.g. when I'm sitting on the platform at the train station), then the immediate challenge is not in learning to meditate or in learning mindfulness (which immediately raises the technical challenges of learning). Instead, the immediate challenge, while difficult enough, is easier than this: Just stop!

The easier first challenge is to stop the habitual urge, the addiction, to do more and more 'stuff'.

Stop the habitual urge to reach for my mobile phone

- Stop the need to check my e-mails again.
- Stop the need to send text messages all the time.
- Stop my need to be doing something – reading a book, doing a puzzle.
- Stop my need to look, sound and feel 'productive' – checking my diary, making a note of things I need to do.

- Stop my need to consider my endless list of tasks, think through my current challenges, check whether I'm supposed to be somewhere else.

If I could stop all of these things for a few minutes a day, if I could work out how to just sit still and not 'do' anything for a few minutes, and if I could learn to enjoy this for its own sake, I'd be giving LittleBrain the well-earned focused rest he needs and craves. I wouldn't be so frazzled.

And this stopping, while fiendishly difficult enough, doesn't require the technical ability or mysterious skill of meditation, mindfulness, tai chi, the Alexander technique, and so on.

Maybe you're braver, stronger, more capable than I am – I find even this unambitious aim difficult. But this is where I've started, and each day that I manage to do it once, twice or three times a day – I feel so much better.

Sitting here writing this chapter right now, in this coffee shop, on this morning, I'm going to do it.

. . .

. . .

There – I've managed ten minutes.

Think about it this way. When I'm sitting here, if I look at the light on the ceiling, my visual cortex is processing the incoming information. I can probably get away with describing the light to myself – the colour, the shape, etc. This visual processing of incoming information by the visual cortex doesn't require any work from LittleBrain. The factual description of the information is being handled by brain regions responsible for processing sensory information and doesn't require any work from LittleBrain (although LittleBrain is feeling the temptation to start saying stuff about the information). But once I start to do more than this, once I start to make decisions and judgments about the lamp (do I like it or dislike it? Which other light fitment does it remind me of? Which of my relatives has a lamp fitting like that in their front room? Hang on, doesn't my boss have a light like that in their office? Yes, I can see it now, just above their desk. I'll be looking at it next Tuesday during my appraisal), now I'm tasking LittleBrain with work. And while it's fairly lightweight work, it's still chewing up more glucose than if I was only processing incoming visual data, without allowing any of this internally generated thinking to begin.

This is the significance of knowing how to stop and have Quiet Time. This is the significance of building your 'skill' – your 'know-how' – to generate Quiet Time whenever you want to.

The amazing power of the beach – I've noticed it while writing this chapter this week (it's July, and I'm on holiday with my family). I step onto the beach and, immediately, LittleBrain goes quiet. I have a total absence of thinking about work, the office, whether my beach mat is as good as the beach mats owned by the family near us on the sand, all the DIY jobs I want to get done at home, whether I should have fish and chips or salad for dinner tonight, etc. Just to be clear, I can get LittleBrain to generate all these thoughts while sitting on the sand, but the strange sense of being far away from the 'stuff' of my life means neither I nor he are as tempted as usual to bother with it all. Instead, I sit and look around and watch people, seagulls, the waves, my kids. And, almost immediately, I'm smiling at all of it – I'm just enjoying it all. I sigh, and move my toes in the sand – magic!

Yesterday afternoon, I invited my children to bury me up to my neck in the sand (something they were much too keen to do!). As I lay there, unable to move, LittleBrain went to sleep entirely. I didn't – I was calmly observing the feeling of the weight of the sand on my body, the sound of the sea, the seagulls flying low over me – instantaneous Quiet Time.

I don't need a training course in mindfulness and meditation – I just need a beach at home! I just need my children to bury me up to the neck three times a day every day!

This is the kind of magical non-think-think-think-calm-observational-thinking that is highly restorative for LittleBrain and for me. This is like the very definition of a day off. It's a day off for my pre-frontal cortex – a day off from the continual think-think-think of it all. After an hour of this, my well-beingometer is going crazy – I feel I've been away from it all for ages.

Then my kids start fighting, my dad asks whether we should have fish and chips or salad for dinner, and the family next to us turns up their music too loud. Ah well, I don't necessarily need a whole day off – several quality periods of stopping, of Quiet Time will have to do the job.

Structuring your day: Four

Give LittleBrain regular quality time off. You don't need days off – quality time stopping for non-think-think-think-calm-observational thinking will quickly produce the feeling you've had loads of time off even though you haven't. It will give a big boost to your underlying levels of well-being.

Stuff you shouldn't do

✖ Don't apologise for sitting still, apparently doing nothing.

✖ Don't succumb to the macho groupthink of no lunch break.

Stuff you should do instead

✔ Schedule small chunks of Quiet Time in your diary. Note them in a different colour or do something to highlight them so they stand out from everything else (you'll need to find tricks like this to use to ensure these chunks of time happen, because you're likely to give them up too quickly in favour of tasks or other activities that feel like 'real work' by comparison)

✗ Don't believe that taking some reflective Quiet Time at regular intervals will decrease your productivity and prevent you getting home on time (take a look at another of our books, Squeeze Your Time, for more about how this can magically increase your productivity and get you home earlier).

✗ Don't fill up Quiet Time with more activity – even if this activity feels fun or enjoyable. Fun and enjoyable activity is absolutely something you should give enough time to, but in terms of LittleBrain and your sense of well-being, it has a different function (one we'll take a look at later). It's not a substitute, so don't confuse them – you need Quiet Time as well.

✗ Don't bring your cat to work and sit there in the staff canteen stroking it (not the kind of weird I mean)

✓ Identify particular spaces at work where you can go to do a bit of Quiet Time. Counterintuitively, public spaces can be helpful; in public spaces, you can confidently do nothing (hiding away can increase your strange but understandable feelings of guilt that you're 'doing this thing'. Also, it can make you look a bit shifty if people discover you – suddenly it looks like you're doing something you shouldn't be).

✓ First practise just stopping – don't feel you need to 'try to do something' in this Quiet Time. Don't feel you need to practise some discipline – this might come later, if you feel you need to or want to. Remember, just stopping might be enough for you. Feel all the different urges to look at your phone, your diary, your laptop, your texts and give yourself five–ten minutes where you don't follow these urges. If it feels weird, know that it's OK – your nervous system is so attuned to receiving constant stimulus that it will feel weird.

✓ If you want to make it easier, you could try paying particularly close attention to something:

– Really take a look at the coffee in the cup in front of you.

– Listen to a piece of music, but really listen to the different instrument parts (resist the urge to sing along – that's not the kind of weird I was referring to above).

– Eat something – but challenge yourself to really taste whatever it is – to really engage with the flavour and enjoy it.

Chapter Ten

Choices – "it's tricky"

You might be noticing how the various activities we're considering here can be contradictory.

When I go to the staff coffee shop, people I know want to talk to me. I'm here to get some Quiet Time, but talking to them will improve my Relationships and this might strengthen my Bedrock Resilience. Which discipline should I satisfy?

What's most important at the end of my day – talking to my partner and investing time in our relationship, getting to bed for some quality sleep, or practising some meditation or mindfulness?

Of course, this is one of the points of this book. The activities *are* contradictory. They compete for your time and attention. So, it's easy to favour one or two activities, and reassure yourself:

> I've got my well-being covered

I remember a lovely lady we worked with a few years ago. We were running a sequence of workshops in her organisation. She'd been a joy to work with across a number of events, when she suddenly stopped attending. Returning six months later, she told us she'd had a breakdown; she'd been working too many hours and had difficulties in her personal life, when one morning she just couldn't get out of bed – just couldn't do it. This lasted a couple of months.

Having recovered, she was really shocked by the whole experience – she'd known she was working too hard and finding things tough, so she'd increased her level of exercise. She said, "I thought that would be enough – I thought that would do the trick. But it didn't."

As should be evident by now, developing and maintaining resilience, resourcefulness and a sense of well-being in yourself is more dynamic than any one of the activities we're exploring. And because they're activities that compete for your time, it's unlikely you'll ever achieve an ideal balance, where you're managing to invest optimum amounts of time in each of them. Your life and the state of things and people around you don't stay static, so it's a continuous project to notice and assess what's happening, on a regular basis, and address again how well you're balancing the various elements that contribute to your well-being. It's a learning task.

Balance is key – balance, rather than completeness – and a mindset that you'll make a small amount of investment in each activity is better than making a huge investment in one or two at the expense of the others.

Chapter Eleven

Externalise thoughts

Remember, two of LittleBrain's superpowers are Memorising and Recalling information. We take these amazing abilities of his for granted because he performs them so frequently and usually quite effortlessly.

For example, LB knows that, in order for you to understand the last sentence, he has to memorise and be able to recall the start of the sentence – by the time you're reading the end of it. In fact, he also has to memorise the previous sentence and be able to recall that as well by the end of the second sentence so as to properly understand what's being said. This takes effort and fuel – you'll notice already that when the sentences in this book get too long, or are badly structured (like this one) LittleBrain has to work harder.

Whenever we ask LB to hold on to information we want to think about consciously, we're asking him to complete two or three executive functions in quick succession – e.g. Memorising, Recalling and Decision-Making. Externalising our thoughts is one significant strategy humans have developed to reduce this strain on LittleBrain, but we don't always make use of it as much as we could, or should.

It's simple, but effective. Here are examples of how humans have learnt to *externalise* thoughts so they don't have to strain LittleBrain by tasking him with Memorising and Recalling information while asking him to do other things with that information:

- Writing – the minute you record something, you no longer require LittleBrain to keep a hold of it for you (it's said Einstein didn't memorise his own phone number, but kept it instead on a piece of paper in his pocket – maybe it's an urban myth, but it's an instructive one).

- Using a diary – when you can refer to your diary, LB doesn't have to keep reminding you about all the tasks you need to get done today (Recalling and Memorising); he doesn't need to keep remembering what it is you're supposed to be doing at 2 o'clock tomorrow.

- Smartphone – if you use one of these, LB doesn't have to memorise and remember all those phone numbers and e-mail addresses. He doesn't have to remember any historical details or bits of cultural trivia you'd like to know in order to impress your friends – he can access all of this on the internet at a moment's notice.

- A hook on which you keep your car keys – once you use one of these, LB doesn't have to memorise where you put them (unless, of course, you failed to put them back last time you used them – darn it!).

- Salt and pepper pots, ketchup bottle, cups and saucers – when someone tries to explain a situation to you by using objects on the table in front of you (how my car accident happened; where I was in relation to the band at the gig; the off-side rule; the final point in the tennis match; how my wife and I met), they're intuitively understanding how they need to reduce the strain on your LittleBrain. "OK, let's pretend I'm the salt pot and my wife is the pepper pot. The ketchup bottle is her boss, and the saucer is my mother. I (the salt pot) was standing here, next to her boss (the ketchup bottle) and my mother (the saucer). Now, as she came round the corner like this..." (moving the pepper pot),

NOW REMEMBER –THE KETCHUP IS HER BOSS

71

etc, etc. They're using objects to represent a huge amount of complex information and detail that it would exhaust LittleBrain to have to recall, memorise and understand while also trying to understand the story they're telling.

These strategies may seem obvious to us when we see them happening or when we hear about them, but it's still surprising how quickly failing to use them can challenge people. Some time ago, I was asked to coach someone who was feeling overwhelmed, was frequently off work with a virus of some kind or other, and showing signs of anxiety and stress. I'm embarrassed by how long it took her and I to find the big solution. We spent some time exploring all kinds of funky options for her to change her approach so she could feel good again, before we got to the problem: she'd stopped using a task list.

She'd used a task list for most of the ten plus years of her career until that point; but now, in a service role in which far too many people continuously asked too many things of her, she'd stopped using it, because she got stressed every time she looked at the huge number of items on it. She had mistakenly concluded that stopping the use of the list would remove the stress.

There are many benefits of Externalising Thoughts – one of them is that once you've made a thought into an object (e.g. an item on a list), you can move that object around and organise it with other objects – and since these objects are really thoughts, this means you're organising your thoughts. Since you're not tasking LittleBrain to do this moving stuff about in the confines of your mind, you're not tasking him to Recall (visualise), Memorise (visualise again), Understand (analyse), Inhibit (stop other items on the list coming into view) and Make Decisions all at the same time. As a result, he'll be using much less glucose, and as a result, he'll be much less frazzled by it.

Rather than stop using a task list altogether, the solution for this woman was to reorganise the items on her list, e.g. move them to future days, so today's list didn't look so large. By contrast, by giving up her task list, she was putting massive strain on LB – requiring that he Memorise, Recall and Make Decisions about far too much information in the confines of that little space behind her forehead.

Starting her use of a task list again, and then using it to organise her thinking was all it took to help her cope again – nothing fancy, nothing stretching, nothing too glamorous, but very significant all the same.

Structuring your day: Five

Externalise your thoughts as often as possible.

Stuff you shouldn't do

✗ Don't task LittleBrain with remembering too much.

✗ Don't think "I'll make a note of that in the diary later." It's so easy to double-handle your thinking by reading an e-mail without writing it onto your task list right now ("I'll deal with that later"), but you're straining LB, tasking him to remember this for you and remind you of it.

Stuff you should do instead

✓ Write stuff down. Notice when you're lazily expecting that you'll just remember everything you need to – you might, but in the meantime, you're working LB too hard.

✓ Organise yourself sufficiently well so you know automatically where specific things belong and where to find them, so you don't have to task LB with Memorising and Recalling utter tat like 'where I put the stapler'.

✓ Sort out your filing system so it works (then sort it again and again so it keeps working).

✓ Review your diary to check how easy it is for you to use quickly and in the moment to get stuff out of your head.

✓ Whatever format you're using for a task list, keep it to hand, in a visual form, if possible, and stay disciplined about recording items immediately – straight onto the page for the day on which you'll complete them.

✖ Don't task others with having to remember too much while you're communicating.

✖ Don't use this as a substitute for listening properly to people (sometimes you need to work LittleBrain harder to demonstrate your interest without writing), but notice when you're starting to overdo it.

✓ Write information down in front of others, e.g. a fact or figure you want them to remember, a choice they need to make between two items (good salespeople do this).

✓ Use objects to represent ideas or information, e.g. a good salesperson puts the product on the table, rather than continually describing it to you. It doesn't always have to be this literal; you can use objects to represent ideas.

✓ Once you've anchored an idea to an object, we all know what you're talking about without having to recall all the detail over and over.

✓ This one isn't just for sales people or in presentations – you could use it in your next meeting, or in a one-to-one conversation you're having. To start with, people think it's strange, but pretty quickly they forget about it because it's just so helpful for them.

✓ For example, in this book, the complexities of the pre-frontal cortex are turned into a simple object – actually, a character: 'LittleBrain'. Imagine if you had to trawl back through your detailed expert knowledge of neuroscience every time you wanted to consider what's frazzling you! That in itself would quickly frazzle you.

Recap

OK, so here's the story so far. LittleBrain is responsible for the significant conscious mental jobs you need to perform through the day. He does this using five abilities: Memorising, Recalling, Understanding, Decision-Making and Inhibiting.

Your habitual ways of working make him very tired very quickly, in ways you don't always realise. As a result, your capability to Make Decisions, Inhibit etc. declines rapidly and more significantly than you recognise. Over time, this tiredness and compromised capability can affect your sense of well-being significantly.

Your compromised inhibiting capability quickly results in a decline in personal discipline, and an indulgence in behaviours that make things worse and prevent you from investing properly in behaviours that would make you stronger and more resilient.

Your use of modern methods of communication and working make things worse. Multi-tasking, splitting your attention, overwhelming yourself with too much information all accelerate the tiredness. You need to reduce the information overwhelm – get more of it out of your head – literally turning it into objects in the real world to reduce the strain. You need to stop the information overwhelm in the first place, but you're addicted, so you seek out more instead – in between jobs, on the way to work, in meetings, on the way home, at the dinner table, during conversations with loved ones, while watching TV, even in bed as you settle down for sleep.

And Sleep – sleep is vital – quality recuperation restores LB's capabilities, but the same addictive drive for productivity and stimulation that is causing the frazzle in the first place, disrupts the quality and amount of sleep you get.

Stopping everything for short periods to get some Quiet Time would help, increasing LB's strength to fight off the frazzle, but your addiction to information, stimulation and multi-tasking make it difficult to settle and prioritise this time. Instead, you may even develop a twitch: the reaching-for-my-phone-twitch or the e-mail-text-Twitter-twitch.

And all of this makes it tempting to de-prioritise the quality of attention you put into your key relationships – one of the bedrocks of your personal strength, further undermining your sense of resilience and well-being.

On the one hand, all this seems fairly obvious; yet, on the other, the subtlety of it, the systematic nature of it, the compulsiveness of the vicious cycle, makes it difficult to spot.

The answer? Take simple steps to improve the quality of one or two disciplines – trying to fix everything at once would simply be too much and could make things worse.

As you read the following summary of the first five of the Baker's Dozen, take a moment to re-evaluate your current satisfaction with each. Mark them out of 100, where one is dissatisfied and 100 is fully satisfied. Notice those that now strike you as a priority to improve.

Sleep: a Rest and Recuperation discipline

While people have varied sleep needs, six–eight hours a night is a good guideline. What's most important is that you start to pay attention to what you're like on less than this.

You go through ninety-minute sleep cycles through the night and each cycle is made up of five stages of sleep. Each stage of sleep has its own particular function for restoring your physical, emotional and mental well-being, so quality full cycles are important.

The circadian rhythm is the pattern of your body's natural, unconscious peaks and troughs of sleepiness, alertness and energy. Too much light or stimulation during the late evening can start to create drift in your own body's sense of this rhythm. This could cause sleep problems.

%

Right Stuff Right Time: a discipline for Reducing the Abuse

The circadian rhythm, suggests heavyweight mental activity is best undertaken early to mid-morning and early evening. The brain has no on-board fuel tank. Tasking LittleBrain with heavyweight mental activity immediately degrades his capability in the same or similar mental activity.

Reduce your multi-tasking, stop splitting your attention between different pieces of information, and notice when you're demanding that LittleBrain understand, analyse *and* make decisions much too quickly. All of these activities increase his level of frazzlement. Even if you think you're really good at them, you'll still pay a price.

%

Relationships: a Bedrock Resilience discipline

Strong social support and caring relationships have positive effects on health issues such as blood pressure, anxiety and stress. So it's important you invest enough time, quality and intention into developing and maintaining them. Going to the pub with your partner to meet friends, or sitting on the sofa together to watch a film is a great Chill-Out activity, but it's not the focused activity required to maintain your key relationships. Find time to talk to each other, to look at each other, to make meaningful contact.

%

Stopping – Quiet Time: a LittleBrain Training **activity**

Aside from the immediate benefits of taking the strain off LittleBrain for a while, this thinking-non-thinking discipline develops LB's skill of Inhibiting. Benefits include an increased ability to resist urges and impulses, a heightened ability to remain focused using less effort, and increased conscious and unconscious power to stop your mind wondering or worrying, e.g. in the middle of the night.

Externalising Thoughts: a discipline designed for
Reducing the Abuse

This key strategy is designed to lessen the Memorising and Recalling demands we make on LB. Writing things down, organising yourself so that particular items and information can always be found in the same place, communicating ideas and data with visuals or with objects are all good examples of simple ways in which we externalise thoughts. Once you've got these thoughts out of your head, LB isn't being frazzled with the business of Recalling and Memorising – instead he can focus solely on Understanding and Making Decisions, which will seriously reduce the strain.

%

It's a system

One of the challenges with these activities is to realise how inter-related they are – what you do in one affects what happens in another in ways it's difficult to identify. This is important to understand, so you don't just fling yourself directly at disciplines you think you have a '*problem*' with.

If you've realised that a lack of quality Sleep is affecting your mental and emotional well-being, it'll be reasonable to fling yourself at all the ways in which you could improve your sleep. But, since sleep is just a part of the system, while you're getting yourself tense about *fixing* this single activity, the problem – or the *solution* – might actually be elsewhere.

If you get to sleep just fine, but wake in the middle of the night with LB whirring and worrying:

1   Part of the solution to your sleep issue might actually lie in LittleBrain Training, and specifically in the practice of the discipline of Stopping – Quiet Time, that is, building your ability to consciously and unconsciously stop the think-think-think kicking in.

2   Alternatively, to stop LB from whirring in the middle of the night, it may be that you need to focus on a Reducing the Abuse discipline like Right Stuff Right Time – addressing issues such as working too late into the evening, or doing demanding mental-effort hobbies till too late in the evening.

If you really can't settle into some Stopping – Quiet Time, it may be that part of the solution lies in the discipline of Changing State beforehand, or it may be that part of the solution is to externalise thoughts first, writing them down to get them out of your head.

If you find your significant Relationships in life aren't going as well as you'd like, improving your Sleep might be part of the solution.

There isn't room to detail all these systematic cross-overs and impacts of one activity or another, but you get the idea – it's a system. And in a system, what happens in one place will affect what happens in apparently unrelated places elsewhere. So, pay attention to the importance and implications of all the activities, and think broadly about solutions.

Chapter Twelve

Confusion

So far, the differences between activities and disciplines have been clear. The five, summarised in the previous chapter, are distinct and different from each other. They even fit into four different functional areas (i.e. **Rest & Recuperation** vs LittleBrain Training etc).

The next few disciplines we'll explore, while different from each other can be confused with each other, and have blurred boundaries between them.

Attention-Span Development %

Exercise %

Fun-Play %

Chilling Out %

A significant reason to make a clear distinction between each, is to make sure you're genuinely giving yourself enough of each of them, i.e. it's so easy to confuse some of them, that it's possible you're not really giving yourself enough of one when you *think* you *are*.

If you can spot this mistake, you can correct the imbalance it might be causing and produce a quick reduction in your sense of frazzlement or a speedy improvement in your sense of well-being – either of which will lead to an increase in your personal resilience.

What defines these activities, one from another, is how you feel while doing them. It's where your focus is, or how your mind is set that really defines what type of activity you're doing.

Exercise: seems self-explanatory: it's activity where the focus is on the exercise itself and designed to make you physically fitter – build muscle, build cardiovascular strength, and so on.

Fun-Play: this is activity where the focus is on fun – and the lack of consequence of what I'm doing. It's specifically designed to produce fun and enjoyment and, in this manner, it is apparently purposeless.

Attention-Span Development – this is activity where the focus is on deepening or improving your application to an activity you find personally rewarding – a hobby or a pastime. It involves elements of learning, practice and sustained attempts to achieve very particular outcomes.

So, as an example: playing table tennis could be defined on one occasion as Exercise, while, on another, it could be defined as Attention-Span Development and on another as Fun-Play – depending on where our focus is – how serious it becomes, how much chat we encourage between points, how competitive we become, how much we laugh, how much we're trying to hone our shots and concentrate on our technical capability, how much we're just mucking about. So, if I don't pay enough attention to how I'm playing, I might plan a game of table tennis to try to relax and have fun, but, instead, what I actually end up with is Exercise and Attention-Span Development.

You might reasonably be thinking **Who cares?**

Well, if you're always playing table tennis in a manner where you're trying to hone your shots and concentrate on your technical capability, you'll be doing some pretty intense LittleBrain Training, frazzling him some more with some intense Attention-Span Development, when you actually think you're giving him a break and just doing physical exercise or larking about with some Fun-Play.

Not only will this easily point the way to why you're feeling so frazzled, e.g. too much Attention-Span Development means I'm working the hell out of LittleBrain, even when I think I'm relaxing – so it's no surprise I'm so tired. It will also point the way to relatively simple improvements you can make (e.g. Play table tennis one less evening per week, and find some genuine Fun-Play instead; or play with somebody different – someone with whom it's bound to be Fun-Play because they're just not up to the technical standard of your play) in order to quickly improve your sense of well-being. Some of these switches of attention aren't difficult to do – once you realise what's going on, you can make the changes easily so you're genuinely getting enough of the different resilience and well-being activities – so you're not accidentally frazzling LittleBrain some more, when you think you're giving him a rest.

We'll look at these kinds of confusions, and how to correct them, as we go.

Chapter Thirteen

Attention-span development

People tend to talk about their attention span in the most absolute terms:

> I have a short attention span

Of course, when they say this, they're not really thinking about what they're saying.

> Concentration is a skill that can be developed

Your attention span is the result of a combination of LittleBrain's superpowers. We've seen that we can help him develop these superpowers further through application and practice.

Hobbies and Pastimes that require you to focus for a period of time, and particularly those that require you to apply yourself to learning, are very helpful to LittleBrain in helping him increase his superpowers.

Learning a musical instrument. Learning a foreign language. Learning to juggle, to stilt-walk, to roller-skate, to ice-skate. Origami. Flower-arranging. Drawing and painting. Arts and crafts of all types. Model-making. Lego. Writing stories and poems. Collecting – stamps, teapots, antiques. Cooking and baking. Playing golf (when you're really working on your technique). Any sport, when you're not just having a laugh – when you're working on your skill levels, practising and refining your approach.

I could go on, but you get the idea. These kinds of Hobbies and Pastimes require sustained periods of concentration, focus and attention.

Of course, we don't take up these kinds of hobbies because we're searching for focus and attention (not consciously anyway); we take up these kinds of hobbies because they bring us enjoyment. It's a very particular kind of enjoyment. As we'll see later, it's not the same kind of enjoyment as Fun-Play (though they share various qualities) and it's not the same kind of enjoyment as Exercise (though, again, they have some similarities).

Specifically, in terms of your pre-frontal cortex executive functions (LittleBrain's key superpowers of Memorising, Recalling, Understanding, Decision-Making and Inhibiting) sustained practice of such pastimes will exercise your muscles in all of them, and particularly in Memorising, Recalling and Inhibiting.

Attention-Span Development brings three big benefits:

1   You'll improve LittleBrain's ability to fight off distractions.
2   You'll improve LittleBrain's ability to re-establish your concentration after distractions.

Both these kinds of improvements will help you to resist the urge to multi-task, and resist the pull of continual partial attention (two things that we've already seen really frazzle poor LittleBrain and make him tired).

3   You'll improve your ability to resist some of your urges and addictions (e.g. it'll help you to fight off the pull of your mobile phone, the chocolate, those digital games, etc).

It's tempting to think all activities that pull on your sustained attention will qualify as stuff that builds LittleBrain's superpowers. For example, you might be thinking, "Video-gaming, browsing through my social-media platforms, watching TV, texting and e-mailing – well, all this requires my sustained attention, so this must be building my muscles in Inhibiting and other superpowers in the same way. This must be LittleBrain Training."

Sorry, no. Let's not assume this is the case. Let's think of the key differences.

The hobbies we're talking about require active internally generated focus by LittleBrain. Social-media browsing, watching TV, texting and e-mailing, many video games – all of these externally *pull* our focus of attention and we passively follow. When you think, "I'll spend a few minutes doing one of these activities" and sometime later you realise you're still doing it, you've got swallowed up in the game or you've found yourself following one link after another, this is a demonstration of how LittleBrain is not generating your attention – he's passively following it. Your attention is being generated by external stimuli. So doing these kinds of things doesn't build LittleBrain's strength or skill – it's not a trip to the gym for him.

By comparison, this is the point of practising Hobbies and Pastimes – they provide LittleBrain Training in this ability to generate and sustain your attention. They build your ability to resist the pull of other stimuli the moment you find things too challenging, the minute you feel the first flutter of boredom.

You might have mindsets about some of the Hobbies and Pastimes listed above:

> Boring

> I'm putting this book down now if it's recommending I take up flower-arranging

Apologies to flower-arrangers everywhere, but it's a fair point.

Boredom is a significant concept here. Boredom is an indication of our need for better LittleBrain Training – it demonstrates a lack of ability to generate an internal focus; a lack of ability to inhibit the thought that there should be something else more interesting available for us – something else that's easier– something else that will generate a focus for us externally. Allowing ourselves to become bored, and then internally generating our attention towards a hobby is really what this particular activity area is all about. These are the kind of muscles we need LittleBrain to develop.

Structuring your day: Six

Invest enough and not too much into your Hobbies and Pastimes through the week.

Stuff you shouldn't do

✘   Just like Relationships, it's easy to neglect Hobbies and Pastimes through the week because you feel too tired to invest.

✘   Don't think you're completely resting LittleBrain when you're investing in your

Stuff you should do instead

✓   When you get home in the evening, take a break before you launch into Attention-Span Development activity.

✓   Once you've allowed LittleBrain some recovery time from the frazzlement of the work day, you should find another burst of energy (remember the second peak of the day in the circadian rhythm).

✓   If you're particularly tired, know that, as with any focused learning kind of activity, little and often can be better than famine

Hobbies and Pastimes. You are resting him (but in a 'change is as good as a rest' manner). Time spent in this state of focused attention is working LittleBrain – in very particular ways.

and feast. Ten to twenty minutes a day will provide plenty of benefits compared with a big splurge of time at the weekend.

✓ Pick the times and the levels of intensity for investing in Hobbies and Pastimes. Again, the circadian rhythm suggests 6pm-8pm is a good time for these kinds of activities. But once you stray past 9pm, you should be aware that you might be stimulating LittleBrain more than is helpful if you're to have a good night's sleep.

✓ On days when you're particularly frazzled, know that investing time in these kinds of hobbies may actually be frazzling you further, depending on how proficient you already are at them, e.g. if you're still learning, you're really going to be taxing LittleBrain (when you believe you're relaxing). However, if you're already skilled and proficient at a hobby, you may not be tasking LittleBrain to do anything much at all – instead, the routine centres of your brain (the basal ganglia) may be in charge, which won't frazzle you further. Again, this is a further reason, during the week, to go for regular and brief investments of time and energy, rather than major sessions.

In summary, this discipline is particularly tricky because it pays great dividends when practised enough and regularly; however, it's easy to push it too far and practise it to an extent that actually frazzles you further without you realising it, robbing you of time you should be investing in other activities (like Relationships) that may benefit you more in any given week.

Chapter Fourteen

Exercise

Exercise is good for you!

You've heard this before? Really?!

Careful with your mindsets about exercise.

> I'm not an exercise kind of person

> Oh no – another lecture on how I need to be active

> I've got this covered – I exercise all the time

It's pretty normal for people to think of exercise as:

- The way to improve my physical fitness.
- A way to help me lose weight.

But exercise's positive influence on our personal state, Bedrock Resilience, and on LittleBrain is much broader than we're usually considering.

Exercise increases levels of the neurotransmitter *serotonin*:

- This affects our mood and our impulse control.
- Levels of serotonin are important for self-esteem.

- Serotonin is a sleep chemical – so levels of exercise have a direct connection to your ability to sleep well (i.e. exercise makes you a particular kind of tired – a sleep-inducing kind of tired).
- Serotonin helps stave off stress by counteracting cortisol (the stress chemical, the effects of which can be both positive and negative).

Exercise promotes the growth of new structures in the brain – structures that directly affect your ability to learn. We'll check in on learning later, but, for now, let's just say that learning is one of the keys to resilience, so anything that can improve your learning will increase your potential to be more resilient[29].

Exercise has been shown to be as effective as antidepressants or psychotherapy in the treatment of depression[30].

Exercise promotes the cellular-recovery process[31].

Exercise strengthens the hardware needed for improved use of blood glucose (remember LittleBrain runs on glucose[32]).

Finally, remember that while you're doing exercise, the brain will be routing your mental fuel, glucose, into the brain regions that need it, e.g. the motor cortex. This means mental fuel is routed away from LittleBrain, which reduces his ability to overdo the think-think-think, giving him a break and a rest. This is why exercise such as walking or running is often accompanied by a quieting of thought – a clarity of thought. So, while exercise tires you, it tires you in a very different manner to the frazzlement of LittleBrain. As long as you don't overdo it, it tires you in a *productive* manner.

So, exercise is good for you; very good for you!

Now, let's take another look at those mindsets:

Stuff you shouldn't do

✗   Don't try to meet everybody else's ideas of what an appropriate level of exercise is. If you set the bar too high, you'll fall short and give up. Some exercise will be better than none. In terms of improving LittleBrain's functioning, some studies have suggested that as little as thirty minutes of activity three times per week could be enough[33] .

✗   If you don't want to turn it into a big thing, don't turn it into a big thing.

Stuff you should do instead

✓   Have a look at what's possible – find the easiest way to achieve enough regular physical exercise. e.g.

✓   There's plenty of evidence to suggest that walking is enough, and of huge benefit to the brain and our well-being[34].

✓   A twenty-minute walk in your lunch hour will re-route fuel from LittleBrain to your motor cortex, and reduce your frazzlement, as well as bringing some of the longer-term resilience benefits described above.

✓   A five-minute walk round your office at regular intervals throughout the day would do the same.

✓   Rather like with Fun-Play, it's about where your head is. Amazingly, some studies indicate that focusing on the fact you're exercising will improve the benefits you get from exercising[35]. So, you may just need to pay more attention when you're moving, walking, hurrying around the office as you go from one meeting to another or as you go from your desk to the coffee machine and back. Switch on the step counter on your smartphone and check just how much exercise you're already doing. Then engage with it while you're doing it, and start enjoying the benefits (it really is all in the mindset!)

✓   Start to spot all the little opportunities for exercise available to you. I've noticed that the two fittest people I know always look for the stairs at work when other people are getting into the elevator. I used to smirk at them and wonder why they were so weird; now I look for the stairs myself and get my exercise while other people are taking the lift.

✓   The two fittest people I know who work in London don't take the Tube or the bus; they spot when places they need to be are only one or two miles apart and walk. I've just started to do the same, and the difference to my daily step count is profound.

Oh no – another lecture on how I need to be active

Stuff you shouldn't do

✗   Don't take this as a lecture. You don't have to take on an exercise regimen if you don't want to – ignore this discipline for now (there are plenty of others to go for anyway).

✗   But don't kid yourself either – it appears that physical exercise is fundamental to well-being, and to preventing LittleBrain becoming frazzled. There's a growing body of thought that we only have brains *because* we move (i.e. that an organism that doesn't evolve movement doesn't have the need for a brain).

Stuff you should do instead

✓   Make your own decisions about what's practical and achievable.

✓   Find ways to make this discipline more enjoyable – perhaps pair up with others. Pair it with Relationship-building, if it makes it more enjoyable. Pair it with Fun-Play, if that helps. OK, so elsewhere I might have said this isn't the right thing to do, but who cares – if it's the only way you can make it happen, do it!

I've got this covered – I exercise all the time

✘ Don't lecture others on how much they should exercise – while your intentions may be wholly positive, it probably doesn't help – they need to find their own way.

✓ Double-check what it is you've got covered:

✓ Make sure your exercise regime is varied enough. Although there's plenty of evidence that walking is supremely useful, there's also evidence that, in order to get the benefits to learning that can be gained from exercise, "it's important to mix in some form of activity that demands co-ordination beyond putting one foot in front of the other[36]." The idea is to complement aerobic exercises such as walking, running and cycling with exercises that will tax the brain as well as the cardiovascular system, e.g. tennis, table tennis, badminton etc.

✓ Or switch between aerobic exercises and more skill-based exercises, e.g. John J Ratey suggests complementing an exercise regime of aerobic exercises with "rock climbing or balance drills[37]".

Chapter Fifteen

Fun-play

Whether you're playing a specific game; whether you're fooling about with your family, friends or colleagues; or whether you're playing a sport with your friends, the discipline of Fun-Play does very particular things for your state, for your bedrock of well-being, and for LittleBrain.

Fun-Play promotes the skill of adaptation; it builds our understanding of the social hierarchy we're working or living in; it develops more flexibility in our emotional responses, e.g. it prepares us to be better able to deal with loss of control[38]; it improves our emotional intelligence, i.e. our ability to perceive the emotional states of others, and of ourselves, and then adopt behaviours and responses that are appropriate for these[39]; and it's a powerful vehicle for learning (in some ways it assists us in *learning* how to learn).

So, deliberate practice of Fun-Play is great for LittleBrain; it's another one of those disciplines that proactively increases some of his superpowers: it's LittleBrain Training – it's going to increase LittleBrain's Understanding, Decision-Making and Inhibiting powers.

All of this is because of Fun–Play's particular qualities:

- Its quality of purposelessness – true Fun-Play is defined by a lack of productivity – a lack of the intention to get *stuff* done; it's intention is solely fun and enjoyment itself.
- Its quality of no consequence – in Fun-Play whether we win or lose has no serious impacts on the rest of our life; therefore, we can use it to learn stuff – often peripheral stuff like 'what's the social hierarchy here?', 'how do I interact with this person while we do this?', 'how do I communicate with people to preserve our collective sense of connection with each other?' (e.g. while I'm beating them, or being beaten in this game), 'how do I cope better when stuff doesn't go the way I want or expect?' and 'how do I learn stuff anyway?'.

I'm referring to this discipline as *Fun*-Play (rather than just Play) because it's so easy to confuse play with more serious mental application in sport, or in your Hobbies and Pastimes. It's important to distinguish, because you might not be getting the Fun-Play you think you are (and, if this is the case, then you might be missing some of the benefits of Fun-Play).

> "Sometimes running is play, and sometimes it is not. What is the difference between the two? It really depends on the emotions experienced by the runner. Play is a *state of mind* rather than an activity. Remember the definition of play: an absorbing and apparently purposeless activity that provides enjoyment and a suspension of self-consciousness and sense of time. It is also self-motivating and makes you want to do it again. We have to put ourselves in the proper emotional state in order to play (although an activity can also induce the emotional state of play)."
>
> Stuart Brown, with Christopher Vaughan, *Play*, 2010, p60

So, for example, when playing golf, with a view to improving your handicap, you probably shouldn't categorise this as Fun-Play.

In truth, it's more like Attention-Span Development activity – and working on your handicap in this way brings you the neurological and well-being benefits associated with a stronger attention span – but it's not Fun-Play, and it's not bringing you the benefits of Fun-Play.

There are many different ways to practise this discipline of Fun-Play:

- Fooling about and goofing around with your friends:
  a) Rough-and-tumble play.
  b) Verbal sparring and banter.
  c) Clowning.
- Specific games: Party games, board games, imaginative games and role-playing.
- Sports – but played with the intention of mucking about, i.e. the play, the fun, the enjoyment are much more the focus than the physical exercise, and this focus is maintained throughout. So, a game of football in which I'm trying to score a certain number of goals, where I get angry with myself and my teammates for the mistakes we make, and I'm trying to run hard and long enough to lose weight is either Attention-Span Development or Exercise – it's not Fun-Play.
- Digging big holes, building dams and sandcastles on the beach.

> "...during play, the brain is making sense of itself through simulation and testing. Play activity is actually helping sculpt the brain. In play, most of the time we are able to try out things without threatening our physical or emotional well-being. We are safe precisely because we are just playing."
>
> Stuart Brown, with Christopher Vaughan, *Play*, 2010, p34

Structuring your day: Seven

Have Fun and Play sometimes

Stuff you shouldn't do

✖   Don't apologise for having fun, and mucking about at work; it's easy to think this is time-wasting, (and it is, if you go too far), but being too serious about everything all the time isn't good for your state or your resilience.

✖   Don't impose Fun-Play on your colleagues at work. It's difficult enough to deliberately practise smiling and laughing by yourself; it's doubly painful when we demand it of others. Banter and playfulness at work require good, strong levels of rapport between colleagues.

✖   Don't be one-dimensional about it. Relentless everyday teasing banter can easily tip into bullying. And don't mistake watching TV together as Fun-Play – it's a different thing!

Stuff you should do instead

✓   Be conscious of actively enjoying those moments of fun that are possible during a busy, focused and hectic working day.

✓   When you're running a meeting, make sure you're not always driving the agenda too hard; notice those moments when you should let the attendees relax, laugh at something, follow an irrelevant line of discussion because it's funny. Pause and join in, and wait before you insist the group charges on with the agenda item in question.

✓   Let people find their own ways to play and have fun. Give them space and time to do it. Notice those who aren't comfortable, and make sure you manage inappropriate or unprofessional banter and fun – this is about helping us all enjoy ourselves more, not about making us feel uncomfortable or harassed.

✓   Don't become formulaic – allow others to lead the Fun-Play as well.

✓   You might need a Pre-Check on your driveway with this one, like you're doing for your Relationship development. You might need to get yourself into a happier, lighter mood before you walk in at night. You might need to make an effort to play games rather than slob on the sofa every night (over the past few years, this has been a major factor in improving my own, and other family members' sense of well-being). You might need to mix it up a bit, to introduce a bit of novelty and interest – don't just keep playing console games together – try a board game from time to time – or a game of darts in the kitchen (OK, maybe not – health and safety!).

Warning: digital-gaming rant – skip this section if you don't want to know!

Stuff you shouldn't do

Don't assume that if you're playing solitary computer games, or games on your phone, that you're 'playing'. There are some differences between Fun-Play and computer play that stimulate LittleBrain differently. It's much like I described in the chapter on Attention-Span Development – the difference between externally generated passive attention span via things like social-media browsing and internally generated focus of attention via the practice of hobbies. Baroness Susan Greenfield, in her book *Mind Change*, describes the difference between digitally generated play and pre-digital play. She describes how, in pre-digital play, the story, the vehicle for play, the mechanism or the game itself comes from you (again, internally generated) and the external props you use – toys, dolls etc – are just that: props. The game is driven by your imagination.

"The point I want to stress is that *you* were the driver and *you* would be in control of your own inner private world, your own inner reality. But now the screen can be the driver. Admittedly, you have to be mildly proactive in turning the device on and navigating your options, but, once you have selected an activity, spectacular cyber experiences contrived by someone else engulf you. You are now a passive recipient, and even though games like *Sims*, for example, allow you to modify and create worlds, it is always within the second-hand parameters of the game-world designer's thinking."

Susan Greenfield, *Mind Change*, Penguin Random House, 2015, p21-22

Stuff you should do instead

Realise that digital gaming – on a console, on your tablet or your phone, is either a **Chilling-Out** activity or a particular kind of resilience activity yet to be defined. Digital gaming evokes its own particular state (and a very particular state in LittleBrain) that could be incredibly good and useful (as in specific brain-training games) or could be unhelpful, for example, overstimulating LittleBrain just before bed, thereby disrupting your sleep pattern.

As with all the disciplines and activities we're looking at, we shouldn't consider digital gaming as intrinsically a good or bad thing – it's a matter of not investing *too much* energy or time in it. You certainly need enough **Chilling-Out** activity to reduce your frazzlement, so go for it, but succumbing to the subtle addiction of it can increase your frazzlement.

Realise when digital gaming doesn't represent the Fun-Play or Chilling-Out activity you really need, e.g. in the past, I've played a couple of digital games that have involved me taking a character through a series of repetitive tasks. In order for me to gain points and progress to a good outcome, these repetitive tasks *had* to be completed *every day* (you'll know the kind of format I'm referring to). After some weeks 'playing', it struck me that the addictive completion of these tasks was really like work. I'd go to work all day, come home, sit on the sofa ready to play or chill out and guess what I'd do? I'd crank up the game and do more work! Work all day, get home and work some more, while thinking I'm playing.

This can quickly become a very 'grey' kind of experience – you think you're Chilling Out, but you're just tasking LittleBrain some more, and the chores you're tasking him with are so mundane and repetitive, you're not having fun – it's just the dopamine hit of an addiction.

Digital-gaming rant over!

98

Chapter Sixteen

Chilling out

Chilling Out is an incredibly important **Rest & Recuperation** discipline. The state of "doing absolutely nothing that has a pre-defined goal", or "being un-goal focused" as David Rock et al define it[40], is like a waking state version of sleep. Chilling Out takes LittleBrain into a version of an off-line state, during which, while he himself is Chilling Out, other less conscious parts of the brain review, refine and integrate the overload of data that's been received and thought-thought-thought about during more conscious activity. As a result, Chilling Out is a significant and necessary component in your ability to solve problems, be creative, make connections and meaning from often disparate experiences, thoughts, feelings etc. Creativity, problem-solving and moments of inspiration are often preceded by Chilling Out.

This one should be easily recognised and easy to achieve. Well, you would think so, wouldn't you! But, it depends on your level of work ethic and, like many of the other disciplines, it depends on your ability to notice what's happening, and categorise the way you're spending your time and energy.

I used to be brilliant at Chilling Out – I used to be a master: Watching movies, Watching TV, Meeting friends, Reading light-weight novels, Reading *Spider Man* comics, watching a football match down the pub.

And when I wasn't working or Chilling Out, I'd be indulging in some Fun-Play or in some Attention-Span Development hobbies. These were the main ways I'd spend my spare time.

But things have changed. These days, I'm not so good at Chilling Out. I've developed some pretty strong mindsets about:

> Not wasting time   Needing to be productive

I guess it's the overdone strength of Squeezing Your Time. I might be tempted to think that it's middle age, but I have much younger friends who seem to have the same kind of challenge.

As a result, these days I can find myself doing something like this: I'll have an evening when I realise I need some Chilling Out. I'll sit on the sofa to watch some undemanding television. But, after I've been watching for five minutes, I'll start to feel like I'm wasting time – I'll start to twitch, and fidget and wonder what I *could* be doing with this time and what I *should* be doing with this time instead. I've been learning to play the guitar for some years, so I'll realise I can do two things at once – I'll get my guitar, and practise a few scales while watching rubbish TV.

Now I think I'm Chilling Out, and I'm not – I'm doing Attention-Span Development.

When this kind of thing happens, by the end of the week, I'll be feeling pretty frazzled. If I have commitments at the weekend, I won't have the opportunity to chill out. By Monday, I'll find myself moaning to my wife and my friends about how tired I am, how tiring *life* is, how I have all these demands on me, and asking, "When will I just have the chance to chill out and do *nothing*?!" It takes me a while to realise I've done this to myself – I had Chilling Out time available and I spent it in Attention-Span Development instead – worse still, I multi-tasked my time, creating dual-task interference and doubly frazzling LittleBrain while telling myself I was resting.

Here's another one: if I'm hanging around the house at the weekend, I'll feel like I *need* to get lots of little jobs done

Need to be productive

And, of course, I *do* need to get lots of little jobs done; but the list of little jobs is endless – I will never complete them all.

If I don't notice this happening, and get a grip on myself, I'll easily end up working all weekend – and not in an efficient, focused manner. No! I'm just nibbling away at bits and pieces in a resentful not-really-getting-on-with-it-properly-stretching-it-out-for-too-long kind of a manner.

Now I'm stuck in between states; I think I'm working but I'm not; or I think I'm Chilling out, but I'm definitely not. I need to be more decisive and do one thing or the other.

But, of course...

if I've frazzled LittleBrain all week
if I've then over-indulged on Friday night with too much alcohol
or not enough sleep (or both)
if I haven't done anything specific on Saturday morning to awaken or refresh LittleBrain...well then, the poor little thing isn't in the right state to be decisive. He's not going to be able to help me. Instead I drift through my weekend in this half-way state. And by Monday, neither LittleBrain nor I have recuperated ready to fling ourselves back into the mad frazzlement of work and the hour-by-hour abuse that I'm going to inflict on him.

You might be reading this thinking "are you crazy – I don't have a problem Chilling Out – I am a master at it!" Sadly, an over-indulgence in Chilling Out isn't the answer either, nor is it a good strategy for alleviating the frazzle. Here's why: if you're too good at Chilling Out, you're not building LittleBrain's capability to resist frazzlement in the first place (you could think of it as failing to build your mental strength). Certainly Chilling Out is needed to deal with the effects of frazzlement, stress and anxiety; it's needed to give LittleBrain time off; it's needed to enable other parts of your brain to process your experiences, and to make sense of things. But, in order for your nervous system to become more resilient, it needs to engage with stress of different kinds (exercise is a type of stress, some foods which are good for us it's now thought may be a kind of stress, Attention-Span Development is a kind of stress[41]). In order to increase his capability, LittleBrain needs to test himself against these different kinds of stress. As we've seen, he needs a broad range of activities against which to test himself, so that none of the particular stress experiences becomes too much.

Trying to cure the stress of too much work with too much Chilling Out may have short-term benefits but doesn't satisfy the need to increase LittleBrain's stamina (or your own).

Structuring your day: Eight

Plan your Chilling Out – and be disciplined about it

Stuff you shouldn't do

✖ Don't over-indulge or under-cook this one – it's easily done. You need to get it just right to get the most benefit.

Stuff you should do instead

✓ Take a look at your diary and make sure you have clear times set aside when you're just Chilling Out. Discuss this properly with other family members, so they don't accidentally stop it happening. By contrast, notice when you're doing too much 'grazing' – just continuously Chilling Out because you haven't defined your time or intentions well enough.

✗ Don't get caught up in too many domestic chores because you're trying to Chill Out at home.	✓ Sometimes, get yourself out of the house for Chilling Out activities (just don't always go to the same places – particularly the pub – a permanently inebriated or confused LittleBrain isn't necessarily a Chilled Out or recuperating LittleBrain).

Pay attention to what you're actually doing when you're Chilling Out

✗ Don't multi-task or split your attention when you're Chilling Out – don't accidentally frazzle LittleBrain more.	✓ Be disciplined – either surrender to the Chilling Out or get on with something else. Switch off the TV when you need to invest a little in your relationship. Switch off the TV when you want to spend some time on your hobby. Then, when you're done, focus on your Chilling Out.

Recap

OK, there's so much going on now that we're in danger of over-taxing LittleBrain, so let's have another recap – let's put the whole picture back together again.

The part of our brain that's responsible for our Memorising, Recalling, Understanding, Decision-Making and Inhibiting starts to use up its available fuel very quickly. And there's no on-board fuel tank to replenish it immediately. As a result, as soon as we begin these conscious mental activities, we become less capable of completing more of them. To maintain optimum mental performance and prevent tiredness, we need regular rest and regular Refuelling. Some of our habitual ways of working and relaxing – multi-tasking, splitting our attention, bombarding ourselves with vast amounts of information and attempting to do too many mental tasks together or too fast all increase the fuel consumption and the tiredness significantly. When we work through this tiredness, refusing to break and failing to refuel, and when we pile on more of the same day after day, we risk overwhelm, and feelings of stress and anxiety caused by the activation of continuous preparedness for fight or flight.

Being disciplined is key. But discipline relies on Decision-Making and on our ability to Inhibit the wrong thoughts and behaviours, yet these are the very powers compromised by the tiredness and lack of fuel.

Focusing on doing the right work at the right times of the day to take maximum advantage of our peak energy would help. Externalising our thoughts with writing or with objects would help. But if LittleBrain is already struggling with his energy levels, we aren't capable of Understanding the situation well enough to make these wise decisions.

Depriving ourselves of enough Sleep, enough quality Relationship development, enough Chill-Out time makes us less capable of coping with the frazzlement we're inflicting; but the continuous on-task energy of our habitual split attention and multi-tasking tempts us to de-prioritise each of these.

We can build LittleBrain's capability to resist the tiredness, to help him become stronger, and improve his ability to maintain discipline. We could practise Stopping – Quiet Time, which would strengthen his resolve to resist information overload and the addictive twitch to seek more stimulation. We could deliberately have some Fun-Play, which would help to increase our emotional awareness of ourselves and others, and build our ability to learn. We could put more time into hobbies and interests to Develop our Attention Span, making LittleBrain stronger and more capable of resisting split attention and coping better with it. But we're easily tempted to de-prioritise these activities – ironically, because we're too tired. On other occasions, if we're particularly driven, we can do too much of this LittleBrain

Training, increasing our exhaustion at the very moment we think we're recovering. Exercise can fall foul of the same tiredness and failure to prioritise, even though it provides so many benefits. And of course, the vicious cycle is that LittleBrain can't make the strong decisions required to change all this because we've abused him so mercilessly.

As a result, it's easy to get stuck doing only one or two of the activities and disciplines that will help LittleBrain and help us. We get fixed with a blend of two or three activities we think relieves our stress, but that is really too narrow to make things better – and could even be making things worse.

Now, check again the key messages from the four of the Baker's Dozen which we've just completed. As before, take the opportunity to update your assessment of your current level of investment in these areas. Which of these strike you as a priority now?

Attention-Span Development: A LittleBrain Training activity

Your attention span is a combination of LB's five superpowers, so you can train him to improve it! Hobbies and Pastimes that require you to take personal responsibility for developing your focus of attention for a sustained period of time can do this. And they produce other benefits for LB and for you: they strengthen your ability across work and life to fight off distraction and re-establish your concentration after distraction. Therefore, like other disciplines, they improve your ability to resist urges and addictions. Crucially, to produce these benefits, they need to be hobbies that require you to generate your focus of attention yourself internally, rather than passively having your attention pulled via external stimuli like social media and some video games which do too much of the legwork for you and therefore don't build mental muscle. Remember, these things are great, but they're more like Chilling-Out activities.

%

Exercise: an activity for building your Bedrock Resilience

Wide-ranging benefits here – enhancing your mood and your impulse control, improving your self-esteem and increasing your likelihood of quality sleep. It can help to counteract or literally burn off the stress chemical, cortisol. It's good for learning and for the treatment of depression as it routes fuel away from LB, reducing his ability to think-think-think, giving him a break. It doesn't take much exercise to achieve improvements – some studies indicate less than an hour each day. Like other disciplines, this one depends on where your intention is – if you focus on the exercise you do while going about other day-to-day activities, you can gain some of the benefits, e.g. if you pay attention when you're walking around the office, this becomes exercise (so, make sure you move regularly through the day and pay attention to this movement when you do).

%

Fun-Play: a LittleBrain Training activity

This one promotes emotional flexibility and adaptation, increasing your ability to deal with a loss of control. It develops your emotional intelligence and promotes higher skills in learning – in fact, it teaches you how to learn. Essential to all this is Fun-Play's qualities of purposelessness and lack of consequence, so it's distinct from the serious practice of a sport or a hobby. Like other LittleBrain Training activities, it depends where your attention and intention is – specifically it requires that you do what you're doing in a spirit of 'mucking about'.

%

Chilling Out: a Rest & Recuperation discipline

This state of being intentionally *un*-goal focused is very different from Fun-Play, where the goal is fun, or Stopping – Quiet Time, where the goal is a focused absence of thinking. This one's essential for providing LB with time off from the heavy lifting – it provides space and time for other parts of the brain to review, assimilate, refine and integrate learning and experience. As demonstrated by famous creative and technological breakthrough moments throughout history (e.g. Einstein was allegedly lying on the grass in the sun when he first envisioned the theory of relativity; John Lennon had been working at a song for five hours when he lay down for a rest and *Nowhere Man* came to him complete; Tom Smith, the inventor of Christmas crackers, had been puzzling over how to put together his festive novelty toy when a log cracking in the fire where he sat relaxing one evening provided the inspiration he'd been looking for). Make sure you provide yourself with enough, but don't accidentally indulge your addiction to certain Chilling Out activities (such as TV or social media). Don't kid yourself that, by itself, it will resolve your feelings of stress and over-work.

%

It's systematic

Remember how interconnected these very different activities can be.

Exercise may be part of the solution to an inability to sleep.

Fun-Play may be part of the solution to a lack of quality Relationships you have with your loved ones.

Attention-Span Development may be part of the solution to your inability to complete pieces of work on time.

Chilling Out may be part of the solution to your inability to complete a challenging piece of work.

Fun-Play may be part of the solution to Changing State and stopping LB getting stuck and falling asleep.

Chapter Seventeen

Changing state

It should be clear by now that
variation of activity is the key to your
resilience and the key to LittleBrain's
capability. If we think of a state as
an entire suite of thoughts, emotions,
mindsets, behaviours, body posture, facial
features and mix of neurochemicals that you're experiencing (or
generating) at any one time, then the reason each of the Baker's Dozen
of activities is included here is because all evoke different states in us
– and those different states benefit LittleBrain and our overall state, or
sense of well-being, in different ways.

Changing State in the ways we've been examining both increases
our resilience and reduces the abuse of LittleBrain. But, when we're
at work, it's not always easy just to switch activities at any moment to
achieve this state change. If you're attending a meeting called by your
boss, they'll quickly find you a tiresome nuisance if you insist on:

- Doing star jumps at the back of the room every half-hour.
  ("Sorry, Boss – I needed to promote an increase in brain
  proteins to strengthen my learning capability")
- Starting a quick game of musical statues. ("Sorry, Boss – we needed
  to get some Fun-Play time to increase our emotional flexibility")
- Having a quick group hug with your two closest colleagues.
  ("Sorry, Boss – we just needed a quick hit of oxytocin")

- Sitting on the floor for ten minutes and chanting "ommmmm".
  ("Sorry, Boss – I needed to stop and get some Quiet Time")

So, it's going to be useful to engage with a couple of principles that explain how to consciously change your state quickly and more easily at any moment through the day.

Movement: humans like movement. You may not always realise it.

> What rubbish – I like lying on
> the sofa, drinking beer!

But it's true – creatures with brains like movement[42].

We know LittleBrain likes stillness – well, actually, it's not stillness itself he likes – it's the lack of split attention, and the lack of multi-tasking that often accompanies the stillness. By contrast, he's not fond of getting fixed. When we get fixed, he's tempted to get bored, his attention and his alertness suffer, and this isn't good for his levels of frazzle. Getting fixed won't necessarily make him more frazzled, but finding ways to perk up his attention and alertness will help fight it off.

Dopamine is the neurochemical of novelty and interest. And movement is an easy way to give LittleBrain a sense of novelty and interest and fire a hit of dopamine. This is probably why people intuitively do things once they're starting to feel too fixed:

- They stretch.
- They yawn.
- They twitch and fidget

These stretchings and yawnings can be useful, but, because of the associations they have, they risk shifting you into a state of:

> I'm bored

> I'm really, really bored – I want
> some entertainment!

And before you know it you're updating Twitter again (under the desk, so your boss can't see).

So, fidgeting and yawning isn't going to be as effective as more decisive signals of change and novelty that you can effect quite easily, e.g.:

- Stand up from time to time.
- Better still, stand for five minutes while you work.
- Move work-stations. Once you've completed a chunk of the work, move to a different desk, or a different chair to start the next chunk (this has huge benefits for learning as well as alertness. When you're learning, your brain orders information into a neural network of connected brain cells, and a specific location will be part of that neural network – making it a different location will make it easier to recall that particular network of information).
- Go to the coffee shop for the next piece of work (or to clear your e-mails).
- Look in a totally different direction for a minute, e.g. look at the ceiling, look at the floor, look over your shoulder.
- Go outside for a breather – quite apart from the physiological benefits of the great outdoors, the novelty of the different air, the different temperature etc. will reawaken LittleBrain.
- Go for a walk (again) – yep, now you're combining Exercise and Changing State – ideal!

Of course, when we're in meetings, some mindsets kick in that, will stop us Changing State.

It's not polite   They'll think I'm not concentrating

I may not be concentrating, but I don't want them to think that!

If we're polite, the most we'll try in order to change our state is twitching and fidgeting – this will work for a while, but in a long meeting, it will quickly lose its novelty value and LittleBrain will drift off into a fug again.

If you're in a presentation or a meeting, it's likely you're already abusing LittleBrain with:

- Too much information.
- Too much complexity.
- The need to Memorise, Recall, Understand and Make Decisions too quickly – or even immediately.
- Too little fuel.
- But on top of all this, in meetings, you and your colleagues abuse him with:
  - Little or no novelty – everyone's presentation (or session) is roughly the same in terms of style, visuals, corporate language and where each presenter stands.

You could make sure the presentations are better and more interesting. But, this isn't necessarily in your control. In any case, we don't have space here to address all the ways you could do this; instead, read a book about presentations (Google one called *Kill the Robot*).

The challenge is to find ways to move so you don't seem impolite or don't communicate that you're not concentrating. Move chairs at each break. Change the way you're sitting in your chair so you have to hold your head in a different position to look at the presenter. Stop looking at the presenter or the chairperson – regularly look around at your colleagues instead. Find a reason to stand up.

Or, if you feel more grown up, just declare that you're no longer concentrating, apologise and explain that you're going to:

Stand up to listen. Wander around the room – but you're still listening. Go for a quick toilet break.

Or, skip all the explanation and just ask for a break.

Physiology: we've already seen how movement can reawaken LittleBrain. If we take the idea a bit further, then even the smallest movements (i.e. changing your facial expression) will wake him up, producing different effects via the associated state change – some of which will further help your well-being and resilience.

Celebrated thinking-skills guru Edward de Bono says: "…if you play-act being a thinker, you will become one…

Adopt the pose of a thinker. Go through the motions. Have the intention and make it manifest to yourself and to those around. Quite soon, your brain will follow the role you are playing[43]."

If LittleBrain is struggling for concentration and interest, it may be that putting your hand on your chin and frowning will be enough to reawaken him. Not only will this fire a hit of dopamine, it will also change your state from what Daniel Kahneman terms cognitive ease to cognitive strain.

> "…good mood, intuition, creativity, gullibility…form a cluster. At the other pole, sadness, vigilance, suspicion, an analytic approach and increased effort also go together…
> …when in a good mood, people become more intuitive and more creative but also less vigilant and more prone to logical errors."
>
> Daniel Kahneman, *Thinking, Fast and Slow*, Penguin, 2011, p69

So, frowning – adopting the pose of a thinker – can be a great way of Changing State to fire interest and novelty, and increase LittleBrain's levels of vigilance, logic and analytical rigour.

But, of course, only if it *is* a change – if you've already spent three hours in a state of cognitive strain, frowning, puzzling, think-think-thinking, then this is not the change in state that LittleBrain needs.

Further than this, fear or stress can provide useful state changes. Momentary fear fires noradrenaline as well as dopamine in the brain. And these two chemicals together, in the right balance, produce mental arousal and attention. Without enough of these chemicals, we're bored, we're mentally under-aroused. Visualising something going wrong, something scary (a presentation to your boss's boss, say) produces the same response in the brain as the event actually happening; we can generate alertness via noradrenaline simply by visualising something going wrong[44].

A smile a day keeps the doctor away: the simple act of smiling improves your sense of well-being. Even if the smile isn't generated by a good or a fun feeling, the smile can itself generate the good feeling[45].

Fake it till it's real

Laughing works in a similar manner.

Smiling fires increases in serotonin, the calming, mood-enhancing neurotransmitter of self-esteem. Of course, this points the way back to disciplines such as Relationships and Fun-Play, because – hopefully, if you do them well – both of these will involve some smiling and some laughing. However, being able to create such a state change, just by smiling, when we're not even feeling in a good mood, is a significant thing to be able to do.

Even in the privacy of your own space (alone in the car, stood in front of the bathroom mirror, or walking round the office) you can get the benefits of a smile or a laugh.

> I can't go round smiling and laughing to myself – people will think I've gone nuts

Well, yes – this is true. If people walk into the toilet at work and hear you locked in a cubicle giggling away to yourself, suspicions will be raised. If you manage it this badly, then we'll need to re-title this chapter "the discipline of being bizarrely eccentric."

You might notice again, that this discipline, much like some others prompts mindsets like:

> What's the big deal?

> I'm not actually doing anything …

Or by contrast

> I just don't have time for this (today).

This is the challenge if you're to create a well-rounded and more systematic approach to managing yourself and keeping yourself in a good state: the small but significant things that make the difference. Don't succumb to doubt or feel, 'I don't feel these are valid things I should be doing in a world that is organised on the basis of productivity, urgency and too much to do.'

> I'm too busy and too stressed today to smile, have fun, walk and sit quietly for a bit

When it's presented as starkly as this it seems a bit silly or pathetic that we might not have time for such simple things, but it's often the feeling we have.

> Even if I had the time, I just don't feel like it

These are the challenges.

Structuring your day: Nine

Take responsibility for yourself and your state

Stuff you shouldn't do

✖   Don't give in to the tedium of overly long or badly run meetings.

✖   Don't stay in the same place all day, locked into the same small screen.

Stuff you should do instead

✓   Take responsibility for yourself; plan for those boring meetings – check in with yourself just ahead of them; and make decisions about how you're going to achieve a regular change of state in a manner you feel is achievable and appropriate.

✓   Establish a routine of movement through the day, i.e. recognise how often you seem to need to move. Know that sometimes a move will help your levels of concentration rather than disturb them.

✓   Move from one place (one room, one desk, one chair) to another as you finish one chunk of work to begin another.

Shift your state in order to shift your mindset

✖   Don't concentrate on how fed up you are with a boring piece of work or a meeting.

✓   Pay attention to the small things you can do to help yourself stay resourceful, and un-frazzled (even changing your facial expression might do it for you).

✖   Don't surrender to being a grouch because you're so task-focused and you need to get so much done.

✓   Pay attention to the lighter moments in the day – they're there, and you have the opportunity to enjoy them more by smiling during them, but first you need to notice them.

✗ Don't surrender to being a grouch because you're tired, sleep-deprived, over-indulged, overworked. It's very tempting and easy to do, but it's a vicious cycle – a downward spiral of cause-effect-cause.

✗ Don't surrender to being a grouch because you're a grouch! It's not good for your well-being, you miserable git! And it's not going to be good for those around you either.

✓ Smile regularly – do it as a discipline, like doing yoga or meditation; smiling takes no time at all (in comparison to most of the other activities we've explored) so bar the fact that we forget to, there's really no excuse for not practising this simple activity (I'm doing it now while typing, and I notice that the stranger sitting across the table from me on this train is looking at me like I might be a little unhinged – ah well, I'll probably never meet them again!)

✓ Hmmmm – the stranger sitting across the table has just smiled back…

Chapter Eighteen

Refuelling

> "What we ingest is also fundamental to how we think and feel. The brain is an incredibly active furnace, consuming 25 percent of the glucose and oxygen we take in. It burns glucose as its sole fuel, and yet it has no storage site for it. What little glucose is present in the brain at any time can be depleted within 5 to 10 minutes if replenishment is not available."
>
> John J Ratey, *A User's Guide to the Brain*, 2003, p368

This is a particularly tough discipline, as there's always so much conflicting information, science, opinion and advice available.

In the past few weeks, I've read that we should eat more meat, we should eat less sugar, we should eat more vegetable protein, we should eat less protein, we should eat less meat, we should fast, we shouldn't fast…and so on.

In terms of frazzlement and resilience, the key idea here is a simple one – don't undertake heavyweight mental activity and then fail to refuel; when you do, you're abusing LittleBrain. Equally, don't expect LittleBrain to perform well if you're undertaking heavyweight mental activity when you haven't put in enough fuel.

A well-known psychological study looked at the effects of food breaks on the decision-making of judges. Eight judges were observed as they made more than 1,000 judicial rulings relating to applications for parole during fifty days over a period of ten months. The study showed that, as the judges made repeated rulings during the course of a session, they would increasingly rule in favour of the status quo. Broadly speaking, this meant that, as an applicant for parole, you'd be more likely to get a positive outcome at the beginning of a session than at the end, i.e. the judge will naturally cope with less complex thinking and make easier decisions as the session proceeds (as his or her LittleBrain gets tired and lacking in fuel). Following each food break, the judges' decision-making was restored to original levels. The study failed to show that food intake was the sole cause of the restoration of full mental powers; however, it concluded it was one of the three possible causes (the others being the effects of a rest – Rest & Recuperation – and the effects of positive mood – the Reducing the Abuse discipline of Changing State)[46].

After this basic notion of the importance of regular Refuelling, the specifics of the best nutrition involved get kind of tricky, and you shouldn't be taking advice about diet from a non-medical professional like myself – you should seek some advice from your doctor.

With this caveat to seek advice from an expert, here are a couple of observations.

1   You should consider whether you're eating little and often enough to keep LittleBrain's supply of glucose replenished.
2   You should consider whether what you eat across the day is balanced enough across the major food groups.

e.g. foods that easily convert into glucose are going to be helpful for LittleBrain – these are the complex carbohydrates – they'll provide a steady and consistent supply (compared with refined carbohydrates and sugar, which will induce less helpful peaks and troughs). Now there's plenty of debate surrounding whether or not complex carbs are good for you more generally; but it's difficult to argue that they're a source of glucose, and therefore a regular supply of them is going to help LittleBrain. In a documentary shown on BBC2 in 2014, *Horizon: Sugar v Fat*, twin doctors Chris and Xand van Tulleken adopted month-long diets for which one ate a high-fat diet (with very little glucose-producing carbs), and the other went on a high-carbohydrate and high-sugar diet with very little fat. In one startling segment, the twins go to work in the City, trading stocks and shares. On the high-fat diet, Xand's cognitive performance begins to wane very quickly, while on the high-carb and sugar diet, Chris's cognitive performance remains strong for the duration. If the quality of your Refuelling leaves LittleBrain struggling in the face of intense mental activity, then it's the quality of your Refuelling that is a significant cause of your frazzlement. To increase your well-being, you need to take another look at your eating disciplines through the working day.

Structuring your day: Ten
LittleBrain needs regular Refuelling

Stuff you shouldn't do	Stuff you should do instead
✖ It's worth repeating. Don't miss breakfast, lunch or dinner through some macho groupthink about how hard we're all supposed to work around here, or through a lack of discipline, and an over-focus on task (forgetting about your Refuelling needs).	✓ Be disciplined about refreshment breaks – they're important. Don't slog through long hours of meetings without taking breaks for food. ✓ If you're really putting LittleBrain through his paces with hefty deep thinking, detailed analytics or creative meetings make sure you consume something appropriate at regular intervals. Consider eating something small just before or just after completing a major piece of conscious cognitive activity.

✗ Don't be unreasonable with your demands for LittleBrain's superheroics if you're following a planned fast or restricting your calories. Don't fail to acknowledge the possible impacts on LittleBrain caused by such disciplines.

✓ If you're fasting, or missing particular meals for health or for religious reasons, make sure you're aware of the demands you're making on LittleBrain – realise that there is an added feature to your level of frazzlement on such days (it's not just a physical effect – it's potentially a cognitive capability effect as well). On such days, you'll need your scheduling discipline more than on any others – you'll need to make sure you're able to do fewer sessions of serious creative, analytical, Understanding, Memorising, Decision-Making activity, and you'll need to ensure you discipline yourself to do such activity at the peak time, as described before.

Chapter Nineteen

Simplification & chunking

Remember, LittleBrain gets easily overwhelmed, and while, if you've trained him, he can be very skilled at dealing with and analysing detail, it *will* make him tired. So, if you're calling a meeting, or if you're contributing to a meeting, a conference or a presentation, or if you're just talking to your colleagues and friends, make sure you take some responsibility for this issue.

In a book like this one, the reader has control over how much of the detail to wade through at a time. They have the choice whether to bother finishing the book or not (of course, I'd be shocked and offended if you didn't complete this one!).

By contrast, in a meeting or a presentation, your recipients often believe themselves trapped while you overwhelm them with a particularly ambitious agenda, crammed with long presentations or discussions full of too much detail and data.

It's the same with e-mail. They're so easy to send that you can just bash out your thoughts to someone without getting clear about what it is you're trying to say. Too often, you'll say in 150 words what could be said in twenty.

John O'Keeffe, in his lovely book *Business Beyond the Box*, described this onslaught of information as "information pollution", but his description was way back in 1998 and things have got much worse since then[47].

A number of mindsets are going to encourage you to increase the level of Information Pollution you inflict on others.

> What I have to say is incredibly important

> I must get my point across

> I must be understood

> They must understand the context, where my thought has come from, the various factors impinging on the situation, and the variables at work, otherwise they'll never understand

Well, yes…but not all the time. Consider instead…

> Not every argument is of equal importance

> Does this really matter that much?

> Is this point really worth the time it'll take me to communicate it properly

> Is it really worth the time it'll take them to understand it

> They don't need to understand everything – I just need to say what's on my mind

But this isn't just about Information Pollution; it's not only about quantity of information; it's about ease of understanding as well. Remember cognitive strain? That's what we're talking about. Joseph Kahneman points out that we mistrust those who use complicated language to explain things that could be explained simply[48]. Like the unnecessary use of the words 'factors', 'impinging' and 'variables' in the last pink mindset. So, remind yourself of some communication truths before you blast off that next e-mail – before you prepare your next update for the team meeting.

Sometimes less is more

Keep it simple

They don't *really* need to know this

What's the key message they need?

And ask yourself...

Do they really need to be cc-ed?

Am I just communicating to cover my back?

Am I just communicating stuff to justify my existence

Am I just creating more Information Pollution?!

Chunking

So many of us know of the famous piece of research by George Miller, first published in 1956[49], which proposes that, owing to the limitations on short-term memory, people will cope with and retain about five to nine chunks of information. Yet so few of us pay attention to this idea when we're communicating.

I like to think of this idea in this way. Consider you write a nine-line e-mail, in which each line forms its own discrete chunk. If the reader does an amazing job of reading your mail, they might retain all nine points (but it's unlikely). Now, consider you write a twenty-line e-mail to cover the same nine points; if the reader does an amazing job of reading your e-mail, they are still likely to retain only the nine points. Now consider you write three pages – still only nine points retained.

A chunk is the information the reader will group together and remember as one piece of information. So, often, what's important about the way you communicate, is not the total information itself, but whether you manage to group it together into chunks so the receiving LittleBrain can cope with less exhaustion.

> It's OK for me to just blather on

> I try to group and chunk what I'm saying

> If I can structure what I'm saying a little, it'll reduce the information pollution

Take a look back at the structure of this book. Notice how I've put it together in a way intended to simplify and chunk a huge amount of complicated information. Each of the thirteen activities or principles I'm covering really requires a book of its own (those books already exist; in truth, this book is a ludicrous summary or simplification of about thirty or more books).

But I consider all this information so useful, I wanted more people to know about it. So, since I'm including it, I've tried to help you, the reader, assimilate it without an unreasonable amount of strain. Not only have I simplified things, but I've created some chunks. I've gathered the huge field of information into thirteen areas, or chunks. If we add the first chunk about LittleBrain himself, that's fourteen chunks in total.

Then, I've tried to get away with this high number by calling the thirteen activities a Baker's Dozen (a pathetic attempt to pretend that the thirteen can be processed as one chunk!).

Since I know this attempt to be pathetic, I've summarised everything at the beginning of the book into four overall chunks:

Reducing the Abuse	Rest & Recuperation
LittleBrain Training	Bedrock Resilience

To really make this work well, I'd probably have to keep putting all the details back into these four over-arching chunks on every page. I've decided that you'd get bored, and feel a bit patronised by that, so I've not done it.

Finally, I've gone for further chunks you can focus on in each chapter:

- The brain-theory bit.
- The mindset bit.
- The 'Stuff you shouldn't do' and 'Stuff you should do instead' bit.

This last-ditch chunking strategy is my attempt to give you a choice of where to focus your attention (i.e. if you don't want to cope with the complexity, you can let it wash over you and just concentrate on the 'Stuff you shouldn't do' and the 'Stuff you should do instead' sections).

Much of this may have failed, some may have annoyed you, or you may just think it's all been said before.

Regardless, if we're to cope with the Information Pollution we're swimming around in, it would be helpful if we'd all put some effort into these kinds of strategies for Simplifying & Chunking complex information – and got better at choosing when to share the complexity and when to keep it to ourselves.

I could carry on with this chapter – and describe what defines chunk sizes, further strategies for simplification etc. Nah...that's enough – it would just be indulgent Information Pollution.

Structuring your day: Eleven

Notice your own indulgence in Information Pollution – simplify

Stuff you shouldn't do

✗   Don't task others to have to remember too much while you're communicating.

✗   Don't fill up endlessly, compulsively on information. Challenge yourself to turn off the news regularly (it's on a loop anyway, so you're just battering yourself with information for the sake of it).

✗   Don't over indulge on social media. With browsing, there's a thin line between Chilling Out and Information Pollution. Even if the information is dross, you might be contributing to LB's frazzlement with more information for the sake of it. .

Stuff you should do instead

✓   People tend not to trust people who speak using long and complex words or too much detail when it's not required. Of course, this is because we intuitively know that it's exhausting for us, and not good use of our mental energy. We want to know that people have the detail available if we need it, but we don't want them to batter us with it when it's not needed. So, work on your own ability to communicate succinctly when needed, whether this is in e-mails, presentations or speeches (or the stupidly ambitious book on resilience and neuroscience you're writing).

✓   Deliberately practise small chunks of time where you refuse to give people too much information. See if you can talk in a manner where they ask for more detail, for a change – because you're not giving them enough.

✓   Really have a look at the ways in which you're doing Chilling Out – deliberately try out some different ways that don't involve exposure to more information and data.

Recap

So, we know how easily and how quickly we abuse LittleBrain and make ourselves feel frazzled and stressed. We need to be strong about doing the right work at the right time of day; we need to be disciplined about Simplifying and Chunking the information we're drowning in; we need to move, smile, frown and Change State regularly enough; and we need to keep finding ways to turn thoughts into objects so we're reducing the strain on LittleBrain. But all too often we don't, because we're too focused on the task, we're too busy following the groupthink of the organisation we're in, or we're already too tired and incapable of thinking about it all clearly.

We make this worse when we don't give ourselves quality Sleep and enough quality development of our significant Relationships, or enough Exercise. We make this worse when we don't give ourselves enough regular quality Refuelling and enough time Chilling Out. We fail to make LittleBrain stronger and more capable of coping with the strain of the frazzlement and stress when we don't invest in enough Quiet Time – focused non-think-think-think time, enough Attention-Span Development or enough larking about and Fun-Play.

It's all too much to get in balance, the wrong things are too addictive, and we're just too tired to bother. And these challenges aren't imagined – they're real – but we're doing it to ourselves.

Here's a recap covering the three activities covered over the last few chapters. Take the opportunity to identify those that seem to be a priority for you now.

Changing State: to Reduce the Abuse

LB doesn't respond well to getting fixed. The mere fact of a lack of variation or change makes him feel tired; meanwhile, you're asking him to perform superheroics. So, develop your ability to Change State in the moment to help keep the frazzle at bay. Regular movement – even the smallest of movements – fires a hit of dopamine, the neurotransmitter of novelty and interest, and this is enough to wake LB again. Smiling increases serotonin, the mood-enhancing neurotransmitter of calmness and self-esteem, improving your sense of well-being even in the face of stress and challenge. So, disciplining yourself to move and smile regularly through the day are two examples of how to lessen the effects of frazzle.

%

Refuelling: a Rest & Recuperation discipline

LB has no on-board fuel tank, so the more you work him, the more you need to refuel. Little and often is safest, and a balance of food groups is most appropriate. Complex carbohydrates are important for glucose production, so be acutely aware of the decreasing capability of LB that will result if, for some reason, you decide not to consume these regularly or enough.

%

Simplification & Chunking: a discipline for Reducing the Abuse

Reduce the Information Pollution you inflict on LB and on others. Pay attention to your impulse to indulge in or show off with unnecessary detail, complexity or complicated language. Whether it's e-mail, a presentation, or just a conversation at the coffee machine – give us all a break by curbing your enthusiasm. And, if you have to communicate a lot of information, pay some attention to how you structure it – look for the key chunks and signpost them.

%

Chapter Twenty

Why's it all so difficult?

Just in case you've missed it in all the detail, let's look at three reasons why it's so difficult.

1   *LittleBrain's functionality itself.* To reduce the abuse on LittleBrain, we have to Understand what's going on, Inhibit our immediate, habitual (easy) responses, and Make strong Decisions. When we're tired after a period of good work, or overworked and stressed from too much, LittleBrain will also be too tired or will lack enough fuel to Understand what's going on, Inhibit our immediate responses and Make strong Decisions. These are the moments when, because he's tired or lacking enough fuel, LittleBrain will feel most like going with the easiest most habitual response. It's a trap – and we'll all fall into it frequently.

2   *It's a system.* Something happening in one part of the system affects something else in an entirely different part of the system – this is difficult to spot. I'm summarising thirteen activities, and they all interact with each other. Your quality of one activity will affect your quality of another in ways that you may not predict. Part of the purpose of this book is to start to help you predict these effects a little more. But it's complex and dynamic, and we know LB won't always cope well with the complex and dynamic. So, as above, your ability to spot what's happening, Understand it and then Make Decisions about it won't always be quick or easy – and this becomes more difficult when you're frazzled.

3   *Routine*. Routine is really important for our good functioning. If
    we didn't develop routines, we'd have to think-think-think all
    the time about everything – and this think-think-think would
    use all LittleBrain's fuel, leaving nothing for Understanding
    and Making Decisions. If you couldn't develop routines, every
    time you switched on your TV or your computer, it would feel
    like you still didn't really know how to make it do the simplest
    functions. Without routine, something as basic as opening this
    book and finding the right page or switching on your e-reader,
    could take up all your mental fuel. Without routine, LittleBrain
    would need to stay in charge of these common and mundane
    procedures; instead, once you've done something just a few
    times, LittleBrain hands over responsibility for such things to
    the basal ganglia. The basal ganglia is a much older part of the
    brain and it takes a lot less fuel to run it.

But there's a downside: because this happens, it makes us love routine.
If we can, we'll turn anything into a routine, so we no longer have
to use mental fuel on it. But, valuing this routine so highly, the
brain doesn't make distinctions between good and bad routines.
So, breaking bad routines, which we've adopted as a result of ease
and a lack of Decision-Making capability (caused by LittleBrain's
exhaustion or lack of fuel) is difficult and takes effort.

Where does this leave us? Three things:

1   Learning – this is the thirteenth of the Baker's Dozen disci-
    plines. We'll come to it in a few pages.
2   Discipline – it's tough, but sometimes, it's all we've got.
3   Routine – streamlining your principles so they become automatic.

When LittleBrain is tired or low on fuel, a key tool available to
us is discipline – the ability to do something even when you don't
want to. But discipline takes huge mental effort. The paradox is

that, to stop abusing LittleBrain, you'll need to abuse LittleBrain a bit *more*. So, discipline is first, e.g. the discipline to make some things described in this book happen even though you and LB don't want to because you're both too tired and frazzled. I've described a number of ways to do this through the book (e.g. the Pre-Check).

By contrast, if you can turn a principle into a routine, then it won't be such hard work – it won't use up so much fuel – because Recalling, Memorising, Understanding and Decision-Making won't be involved. For a routine to kick in, the most that might be needed is Inhibiting – Inhibiting the automatic start-up of an old routine so a new one can start in its place. That's right: bad routines (habits) stay in your basal ganglia – they don't go away. So one of the only ways to stop them is to cement a new routine into the basal ganglia to crowd them out[50].

There are two ways to do this. The first is practise. As mentioned before, sometimes it takes as little as three uses of a new behaviour or thought, before it becomes routine – but this isn't always the case – maybe it depends on the strength of the existing routine, already in the basal ganglia that you're trying to crowd out. One way or another, repetition is the key.

Another key is to turn a principle into a routine by stating it as a "process goal". Process goals are very specific types of goal – they're sometimes described as "thoughts to live by"[51], and they're typically designed to pull our attention back to something about our current behaviour that we want to focus on (a strength we want to make more of, or a blind spot we want to be more aware of). They're often mindsets. This book has plenty of process goals in it.

Here's a quick example of how it works. If I turn a principle of I need to walk more into a process goal, I'll make it SMART (specific, measureable, achievable, realistic and with a timescale), e.g. I take the stairs on every occasion that others take the lift.

It's in the SMART qualities that the principle becomes a routine – with a SMART process goal, it's almost like the instruction goes straight to the basal ganglia. The vagueness of "I need to walk more" means LB has to think-think-think and Make Decisions when confronted with the elevator. The SMART-ness of "I take the stairs when others take the lift" means no Recalling, Memorising, Understanding or Decision-Making is required from LB. All that's needed is Inhibiting long enough for "I take the stairs" to be pulled from the basal ganglia – once this happens, I know what I'm doing.

Chapter Twenty-One

Putting it all together

We're very nearly done. I hope, as we approach the finish, that you'll keep remembering that this is all about making small but significant shifts in your daily and weekly activities and routines. Meanwhile, attempt to do four things:

You could simply start to work on your resilience and well-being at this top-line level – consider everything we've explored, and identify which one of these four you need to work on first.

For example, as I've been writing this book over the past six months, I've realised (sometimes quite slowly) that I do abuse LittleBrain on a regular basis, but currently this isn't my biggest need. I'm all too good at LittleBrain Training – I'm regularly putting him through his paces – often till too late in the evening, and often, replacing one form of demanding mental activity with another. My Bedrock Resilience comes and goes, but over those six months, I've been disciplined enough for this not to be my biggest need. My biggest need right now is Rest & Recuperation, and that's what I'm working to improve at the moment.

I'm hopeful that even if you only complete this type of surface-level analysis, using the four big chunks, you'll be able to make some noticeable improvements to your sense of well-being.

If you want to go deeper, you should be able to develop a more detailed diagnosis via the Baker's Dozen disciplines, paying attention to the way some cross over with others.

So, for example, at the time of writing, my diagnosis for myself is:

1   I need to get better at Rest & Recuperation – specifically, I need to improve the quality of my Sleep; and I need to get more disciplined with my Chilling Out.

2   In order to improve the quality of my Sleep, I need to:
    a) Make my Exercise more regular – I don't need very much to make a difference, but I need a small amount every day to tire me enough to keep me asleep through the night.
    b) I need to give myself more LittleBrain Training in the discipline of Stopping – Quiet Time. I can usually fall asleep OK, but if I wake at the end of a sleep cycle, LittleBrain starts to whirr. Since I've already stopped exposing him to light and too much stimulation later in the evening, it's increasingly clear to me that I need to practise meditation, so LittleBrain improves his Inhibiting and is able to turn off the think-think-think at 3am.

3   I'm still all too capable of abusing LittleBrain throughout the day, so, during the writing of this book, I've paid attention to the decisions I make about what activity and work to do at which times of the day, and this has helped me no end.

4   While I'm generally very good at Changing State – moving work-stations as I finish one piece of work to begin another – I've noticed I've more to do here. Specifically, when I'm engaged in a longer piece of work, (like a writing day), without the sense of progressing from one piece of work to another,

I get fixed – and I get frazzled. I need to move regularly, even if it's just from one chair to another at the same table.

That's plenty, so I'll be working on these things for the next three months, before I re-read the book (yes, I know I wrote it, but I'll still forget huge amounts of it – LB doesn't want to hold all that in the tiny space behind my forehead). I'll review my success levels and identify my priorities again in three months. For those of you thinking I'm not being honest, and there's bound to be more I should be focusing on – you're correct, there is more – but, of course, if I focus on too much at once, I'll just overload LB, and that'll add to the frazzle again.

Sweet spots

At regular intervals, I've emphasised how easy it is to mistake one activity for another, e.g. thinking I'm giving myself some Fun-Play when I'm actually doing Attention-Span Development. Without doubt, this is the important principle to keep in mind.

But, the opposite is also true: there are activities that, if I do them in a particular manner, will deliver on multiple areas at once. Here are a couple of examples to get you thinking:

Table tennis. I've seen studies on TV that suggest this particular game is very good for reducing the negative effects of ageing. This is because, when played in a social-club situation, it combines the benefits of Exercise, Fun-Play and Relationships. In fact, these studies indicate that its particular contribution to slowing the ill effects of the natural ageing process are strongest in the reverse order, i.e. the biggest benefit comes from how it acts as a Relationship development activity, then as Fun-Play and, lastly, as Exercise. By comparison, apparently similar activities such as tennis are much stronger on the Exercise element and fail to deliver significantly on the Relationships and Fun-Play elements.

Singing. Joining a choir has obvious multiple benefits in a similar manner. It provides good levels of LittleBrain Training in its requirement to learn, practise and master particular songs and singing techniques. But it also provides major Relationships activity as it promotes such regular social occasions (good choirs rarely go straight home once they've finished the singing). The act of singing is a Changing State activity, producing physiological benefits via breathing exercises and the act of smiling, both at your audience and your fellow singers. And finally, and paradoxically, one could probably make the case for this as a form of Stopping – Quiet Time activity in that, once everyone's learnt their part and their technique and the whole choir is in a state of flow, LittleBrain will fall silent and you'll be swept up in a state of energising mental stillness and euphoria, which could last for any number of songs.

There are going to be plenty of sweet spots like these available. Once you've really got the distinctions of the Baker's Dozen disciplines clear, you can start to notice and develop them.

Chapter Twenty-Two

Learning

This last of the Baker's Dozen is more of a principle or a mindset than an activity.

The psychologist Carol Dweck has been researching the significance of this one for over forty years. In her wonderful book *Mindset*[52], she describes how people's motivation is defined by their adoption of one of two broad mindsets:

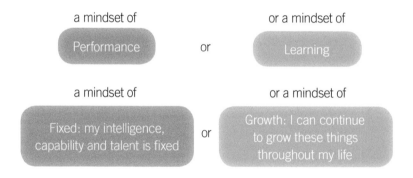

a mindset of **Performance** or a mindset of **Learning**

a mindset of **Fixed: my intelligence, capability and talent is fixed** or a mindset of **Growth: I can continue to grow these things throughout my life**

The significance to our story here is profound: Dweck's research indicates that the sustained adoption of the blue mindsets (the sustained shift out of the pink ones and into the blue ones), by itself, creates in people "the love of challenge, belief in effort, resilience in the face of setbacks, and greater (more creative!) success[53]." Why? Because the sustained shifts from the Performance and Fixed mindsets into the Learning and Growth mindsets "change what people strive for and what they see as success...they change the definition, significance, and impact of failure. And…they change the deepest meaning of effort[54]."

> "Even in the growth mindset, failure can be a painful experience. But it doesn't define you. It's a problem to be faced, dealt with, and learned from."
>
> Carol Dweck, *Mindset*, 2012, p32

In terms of resilience, the big news is the blue mindsets help you to process failure differently (not consciously – so, once you've got it, it doesn't require so much energy of LittleBrain). If you read biographies of great achievers, like Isambard Kingdom Brunel, Thomas Edison, Anita Roddick, James Dyson, Tanni Grey-Thompson, Walt Disney or Mahatma Gandhi, it doesn't take many pages for their habitual use of the Growth and Learning mindsets to become evident. It doesn't take long to realise that their learning mindsets are one of a number of key pillars in their phenomenal levels of resilience. Accordingly, they process major failures as merely part of a much longer story – and they certainly don't consider *themselves* the failure. Instead, failure is something that happens, and when it does, they typically take very specific learning from it and use this learning as the motivation, the know-how or even the solution to their next project, or their next attempt at the same project.

Sound simple? It *is* simple, if you're already habitually using the Growth and Learning mindsets. But if you're in the Fixed and Performance mindsets, then it's not. Like all mindsets, they usually operate at an unconscious level, so, to change them, you need to think about them, notice what's happening and deliberately, consciously train yourself to shift into the blue mindsets.

For this reason, I could have categorised this discipline as LittleBrain Training because it'll require you to *train* him in a very particular thought process. In the short term, it will be a strain on LittleBrain – another think-think-think for him to perform regularly. But, the aim is to shift this think-think-think into the basal ganglia as soon as possible – to make it routine – at which point, LittleBrain shouldn't be involved very often; it becomes unconscious Bedrock Resilience.

The choice between Performance and Learning, Fixed and Growth is really a much larger number of mindset choices (Dweck describes many in her book).

For example, it's the choice between:

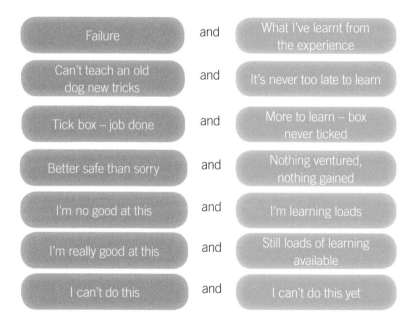

Failure	and	What I've learnt from the experience
Can't teach an old dog new tricks	and	It's never too late to learn
Tick box – job done	and	More to learn – box never ticked
Better safe than sorry	and	Nothing ventured, nothing gained
I'm no good at this	and	I'm learning loads
I'm really good at this	and	Still loads of learning available
I can't do this	and	I can't do this yet

This might look like positive thinking; it's not. To engage with learning, you're going to have to engage with failure. To engage with learning, you're going to have to engage with the fact that you're 'no good at this yet'. It takes effort to remorselessly keep going for the Growth and Learning mindsets.

At the moment that I'm writing this sentence, I've been learning electric guitar for ten years. At the beginning, I wasn't really trying – I was sitting in with my children, while they learnt. Pretty quickly, I was better at guitar than I ever wanted to be. I kept going, putting in only enough practice to keep improving. Then, three years ago, my aspiration changed – I started to learn for myself, I started to apply myself properly. I continue to be *way beyond* what I ever wanted to be able to do with the electric guitar, but I haven't ticked the box – there's so much more to learn and I still can't do what I'd like to be able to do when I pick it up. The level of practice I'm going for now takes more effort – effort I don't often have on a weekday night, if I surrender to the laziness (and let's be honest, I'm not practising very much – I could do much more). A friend of mine who's played the guitar for forty years, who's been in many bands and been a semi-professional musician, said all the same stuff to me recently. He's amazing on the guitar, but he said to me, "I can't yet do what I want to be able to do." He's still learning – and to do so, he's having to put the effort in over the long term.

Of course, I've been saying this since the very beginning of this book. To have the life you want, to have the sense of well-being you want, to feel as resilient as you want to feel takes effort, and work. And this attitude itself, this mindset of...

> Effort and work over the
> long term is what it takes

> Effort and work over the long
> term is what I'm signing up for

even

> Effort and work over the
> long term is good

This is key – this is a constituent part of Professor Dweck's Growth and Learning mindset.

Learning is fundamental to improving your well-being and resilience. As I've said before, it's unlikely you're ever going to get the balance of the Baker's Dozen disciplines just right – the situation, the state of others, what's going on will change around you, so your mix of activities stops working. Observing this, noticing what's happening, Making Decisions about it, and making changes – this will take the hard work of learning – actually this *is* learning!

That's it for now...

It's been very difficult to keep this book tidy, and to finish it at all. There's so much I've left out.

There are significant topics I've resisted the urge to cover at all. It would be easy to write the same amount again from a number of perspectives:

- How to manage my team via these principles.
- How to use these principles to make me a better manager.
- Understanding how I manage LittleBrain at School.
- LittleBrain parenting principles.

Maybe, once I've recovered from the frazzlement of this project, I'll get cracking on these books as well. They'll have titles like *Don't Drain Team LittleBrain*, *Why's School Uncool?*, and *Parenting LittleBrain*. Consider my copyright established!

I'm resisting the temptation to type any more now, though – after all that, your own LittleBrain must be frazzled!

I know mine is...

Bibliography

Peta Bee, 'Kiwi fruit and other secrets to sleeping well', *The Times 2*, Tuesday 11 October 2016, p6-7

James A Blumenthal PhD, Patrick J Smith PhD, and Benson M Hoffman, PhD, 'Is exercise a viable treatment for depression?', *ACSMs Health Fit J.* July/August, 2012

Michael Bond, 'Everybody Say Omm', *New Scientist*: The Collection Issue Three – A Better You, Reed Business Information Ltd, 2014, p24-27

Stuart Brown, with Christopher Vaughan, *Play – How it Shapes the Brain, Opens the Imagination and Invigorates the Soul*, Avery, 2010

Benedict Carey, *How We Learn*, Macmillan, 2014

Shai Danziger, Jonathan Levav & Liora Avnaim-Pesso, 'Extraneous Factors in Judicial Decisions', Proceedings of the National Academy of Sciences 108, 26 April 2011. Published online 11 April 2011

Edward de Bono, *Six Thinking Hats*, Penguin, 1985

Norman Doidge, *The Brain that Changes Itself*, Penguin, 2007

Charles Duhigg, *The Power of Habit*, Random House, 2013

Susan Greenfield, *Mind Change*, Penguin Random House, 2015

Jonathan Haidt, *The Happiness Hypothesis*, Arrow, 2006

Jessica Hamzelou, 'Retune Your Immune System', *New Scientist*: The Collection Issue Three – A Better You, Reed Business Information Ltd, 2014, p119-123

Daniel Kahneman, *Thinking, Fast and Slow*, Penguin, 2011

Daniel J Levitin, *The Organized Mind*, Dutton, 2015

Paul Martin, *Counting Sheep*, Flamingo, 2002

Philipp Mergenthaler, 'Ute Lindauer and Andreas Meisel, Sugar for the brain: the role of glucose in physiological pathological brain function', *Trends Neurosci*, October 2013; 36(10), p587-597

George Miller, Psychological Review, vol 63, 1956, p81-97

Sergio Pellis and Vivien Pellis, *The Playful Brain*, One World Publications, 2010

John J Ratey, MD, *A User's Guide to the Brain*, Abacus, 2003

John J Ratey & Eric Hagerman, *Spark, How Exercise Will Improve the Performance of Your Brain*, Quercus, 2009, p53-54

David Rock, *Your Brain at Work*, HarperCollins, 2012

David Rock, Daniel J Siegel, Steven AY Poelmans & Jessica Payne, 'The Healthy Mind Platter', *NeuroLeadership Journal*, Issue Four, October 2012

Dr Bob Rotella, with Bob Cullen, *The Golfer's Mind*, Pocket Books, 2007

Simon Sinek, *Leaders Eat Last*, Portfolio Penguin, 2014

Caroline Williams, 'Don't swallow them', *New Scientist*: The Collection Issue Three – A Better You, Reed Business Information Ltd, 2014, p45-48

Richard Wiseman, *Night School, The Life-Changing Science of Sleep*, Pan Books, 2015

Richard Wiseman, *59 Seconds*, Pan Macmillan, 2010

Endnotes

1   Daniel J Simons & Christopher Chabris, 'Gorillas in our midst: sustained inattentional blindness for dynamic events.' Perception, vol 28, 1999, p1059-1074 (http://www.wjh.harvard.edu/~cfc/Simons1999.pdf

2   Daniel J. Levitin, *The Organized Mind*, Viking, 2015

3   Carol Dweck, *Mindset*, Robinson, 2012

4   Richard Wiseman, *Did You Spot the Gorilla?*, Arrow, 2004

5   Peta Bee, 'Kiwi fruit and other secrets to sleeping well', The Times 2, 11 October 2016, p6-7

6   Richard Wiseman, *Night School: the life-changing science of sleep*, Pan, 2015 p71-72

7   Paul Martin, *Counting Sheep*, Flamingo, 2003, p89-106, and Richard Wiseman, *Night School, The Life Changing Science of Sleep*, Pan Books, 2015, p28-32

8   Richard Wiseman, *Night School, The Life-Changing Science of Sleep*, Pan Books, 2015, p39

9   Ibid, p39

10   Paul Martin, *Counting Sheep*, Flamingo, 2003, p116

11   Peta Bee, 'Kiwi fruit and other secrets to sleeping well', The Times 2, 11 October 2016, p7

12   Richard Wiseman, *Night School, The Life-Changing Science of Sleep*, Pan Books, 2015, p175-176

13   Richard Wiseman, *Night School, The Life-Changing Science of Sleep*, Pan Books, 2015, p174-175

14   Luis Villazon, BBC Science Focus, #300, November 2016, p98

15 Jessica Hamzelou, 'Retune Your Immune System', New Scientist: The Collection Issue Three – A Better You, Reed Business Information, 2014, p121

16 Simon Sinek, *Leaders Eat Last*, Portfolio Penguin, 2014, p49–50

17 Simon Sinek, *Leaders Eat Last*, Portfolio Penguin, 2014, p47–49

18 John J Ratey, *A User's Guide to the Brain*, Abacus, 2003, p236

19 John J Ratey and Eric Hagerman, *Spark*, Quercus, 2009, p77–84

20 John J Ratey and Eric Hagerman, *Spark*, Quercus, 2009, p42–53

21 Simon Sinek, *Leaders Eat Last*, Portfolio Penguin, 2014, p49–52

22 David Rock, Daniel J Siegel, Steven AY Poelmans & Jessica Payne, 'The Healthy Mind Platter', NeuroLeadership Journal, Issue Four, October 2012, p12-13

23 Michael Bond, 'Everybody Say Om', New Scientist: The Collection Issue Three – A Better You, Reed Business Information Ltd, 2014, p25

24 Ibid, p25

25 Ibid, p25

26 Ibid, p26

27 Ibid, p26

28 Ibid, p27

29 John J Ratey and Eric Hagerman, *Spark*, Quercus, 2009, p42-53

30 James A Blumenthal PhD, Patrick J Smith PhD and Benson M Hoffman PhD, 'Is exercise a viable treatment for depression?', ACSMs Health Fit J. 2012 July/August, 14-21

31 John J Ratey and Eric Hagerman, *Spark*, Quercus, 2009, p78

32 John J Ratey and Eric Hagerman, *Spark*, Quercus, 2009, p78

33 John J Ratey and Eric Hagerman, *Spark*, Quercus, 2009, p55

34 Norman Doidge, *The Brain that Changes Itself*, Penguin, 2007, p252

35 Richard Wiseman, *59 Seconds*, Pan Macmillan, 2010, p199-200

36 John J Ratey and Eric Hagerman, *Spark*, Quercus, 2009, p55

37 Ibid, p55

38 David Rock, Daniel J Siegel, Steven AY Poelmans & Jessica Payne, 'The Healthy Mind Platter', NeuroLeadership Journal, Issue Four, October 2012, p7

39   Stuart Brown, with Christopher Vaughan, *Play*, Avery, 2010, p32

40   David Rock, Daniel J Siegel, Steven AY Poelmans & Jessica Payne, 'The Healthy Mind Platter', NeuroLeadership Journal, Issue Four, October 2012, p8

41   Caroline Williams, 'Don't swallow them', New Scientist: The Collection Issue Three – A Better You, 2014, Reed Business Information Ltd, p47

42   John J Ratey, *Spark*, Quercus, 2009, p40

43   Edward de Bono, *Six Thinking Hats*, Penguin, 1985, p6-7

44   David Rock, *Your Brain at Work*, HarperCollins, 2012, p64-65

45   Richard Wiseman, *59 Seconds*, Pan Macmillan, 2010, p32-33

46   Shai Danziger, Jonathan Levav & Liora Avnaim-Pesso, 'Extraneous Factors in Judicial Decisions', Proceedings of the National Academy of Sciences 108, 26 April 2011. Published online 11 April 2011

47   John O'Keeffe, *Business Beyond the Box*, Nicholas Brealey, 1999, p65

48   Daniel Kahneman, *Thinking, Fast and Slow*, Penguin, 2011, p63

49   George Miller, Psychological Review, vol 63, p81-97, 1956

50   Charles Duhigg, *The Power of Habit*, Random House, 2013, p20-21

51   Dr Bob Rotella in *The Golfer's Mind*, lists 'Thoughts to Play By', which are lists of process goals

52   Carol Dweck, *Mindset*, Robinson, 2012

53   Carol Dweck, *Mindset*, Robinson, 2012, p12

54   Ibid, p12

Acknowledgements

Sometime in the last few years, my friend Luke suggested I read *The Healthy Mind Platter,* by David Rock, Daniel J Siegel, Steven A Y Poelmans & Jessica Payne. I'd been working on issues of personal resilience and well-being for at least 15 years by then – training and coaching people on how to look after themselves better, whilst getting more of what they wanted at work.

This wonderful article pulled together so many of the disparate ideas I'd been working on and put them all in one place. It really crystallised for me the idea that there **could be** a set of everyday activities - that most of us already do – which profoundly affect our resilience and well-being in very scientific ways. I wanted to understand this science better so that I could use it to improve my well-being further. I started applying the ideas to myself and my own disciplines, I started discussing the ideas with everybody I met. I read more.

Once the mindset was in place, I noticed the ideas everywhere – the learning principles I'd been using in the training room for years, were suddenly re-cast in the context of resilience and well-being. Ideas about how the Pre-Frontal Cortex works were popping up everywhere from the BBC programme, Horizon: Sugar Vs Fat, through Daniel Kahneman's *Thinking Fast & Slow* to David Rock's fantastic *Your Brain at Work.*

The Healthy Mind Platter described 7 everyday activities. As I played with my own disciplines, the everyday activities expanded into the 13 I've described. And as I discussed and played with the ideas, I noticed the personal challenges involved, the conflicts involved, the thinking traps involved, the hard work involved. I noticed that very few of the people I spoke to seemed to have much awareness of the significance of the Pre-Frontal Cortex and the importance of the everyday resilience activities – not a surprise, as I'd only just found out about it myself. I felt a burning need for more people to understand this information. But very few that I talked to wanted to read the amount I was reading. As I discussed it, I found myself simplifying everything into smaller chunks in order to make it more accessible for more people. This book, designed to simplify the science, gather everything into one place and explore the challenges – began to write itself.

I've tried hard to make sure I've referenced all sources I've made use of. But, those that really got me excited and inspired to read more and pull together my own thinking about this fascinating topic were Benedict Carey, *How we learn*, Johnathan Haidt, *The Happiness Hypothesis*, Daniel J Levitin, *The Organised Mind*, Dr. John J Ratey & Eric Hagerman, *Spark, How Exercise Will Improve the Performance of Your Brain*, David Rock, *Your Brain at Work*, and David Rock et al, *The Healthy Mind Platter*. I can't recommend these works highly enough.

Thanks to Doug Richardson, my friend, business partner and the co-developer of so much over so many years. Thanks to Alison Rogers, Andrew Manuel and Luke Thomas, conversations with whom have contributed in all kinds of ways.

And thanks to my wife Jo, and my children, Emma, Jacob, Harriet and Jacob, who all had to put up with my excited ramblings during the process (and still have to now!).

Lightning Source UK Ltd.
Milton Keynes UK
UKHW05f2105290318
320242UK00009BA/101/P